Ghislaine Howard

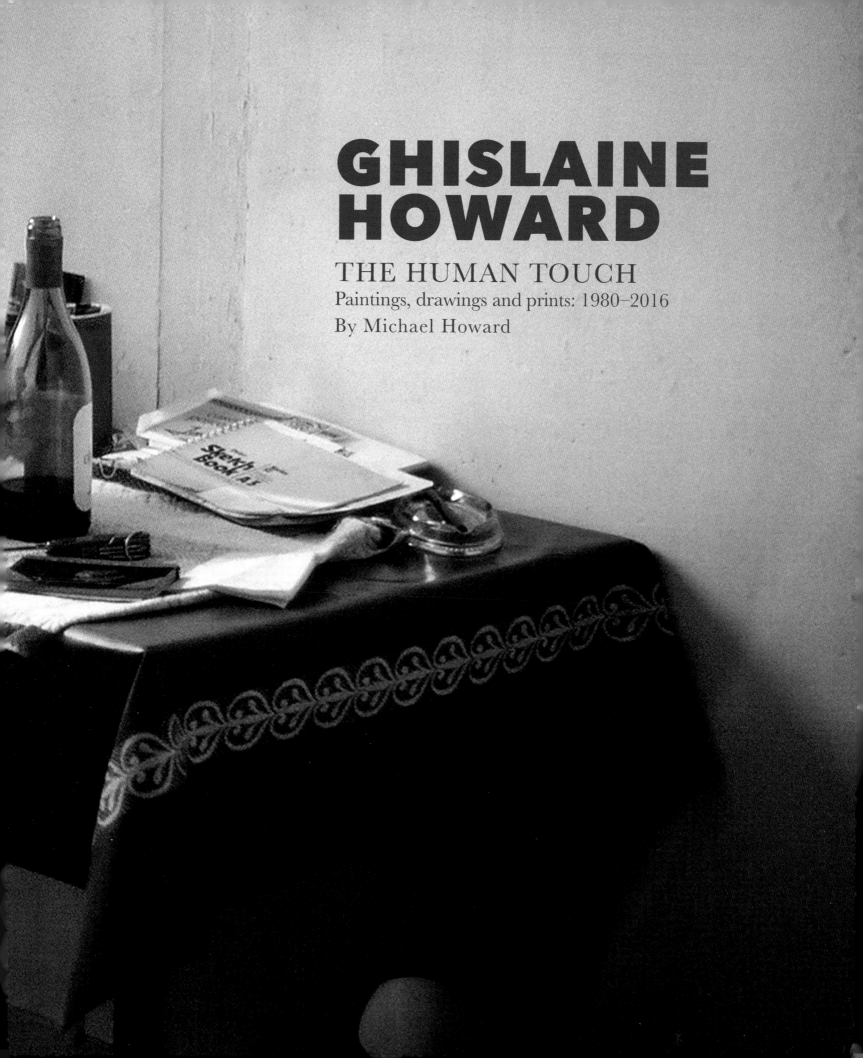

GHISLAINE HOWARD

THE HUMAN TOUCH
Paintings, drawings and prints: 1980–2016
By Michael Howard

Naked Self-Portrait Drawing
2014
Graphite and wash on paper
22.8 x 15.25 cm
Collect Art

Ghislaine at the Table
(previous)
1981
Belle-Île-en-Mer
Photograph by Michael Howard

This book is dedicated to the memory of Maureen 'Mo' Dobson,
indomitable and much loved: a woman of spirit.

'If I read a book and it makes my whole body so cold no fire can warm me,
I know *that* is poetry.
If I feel physically as if the top of my head were taken off,
I know *that* is poetry.
These are the only ways I know it.
Is there any other way?'

Emily Dickinson[1]

A few words from **Martin Heaps**

I first met Ghislaine when a fellow dealer and friend invited me to accompany him on a visit to Ghislaine's studio at her house in Glossop. Upon first meeting her I tried to behave in my usual professional manner, but couldn't help my eyes ranging over the work that was stacked behind her and hanging along the studio walls. In particular I remember seeing a large figurative piece, and as I was trying to concentrate on what Ghislaine was saying, all I could hear inside my head was 'Wow!' I knew instantly that here was an artist whose work operated on a totally different level to any I had seen before.

The main thing I look for when I first see an artist's work is originality, and I found it here. Then I look for feeling – and with Ghislaine's work you can immediately feel the passion. For me, this is the mark of a great artist: the ability to express feelings in paint and once an artist can deliver this kind of work, their paintings become living things.

I feel that Ghislaine is one of the most important and original artists working today. Her own vision, compassion and skill make her paintings stand out in any of the many prestigious venues in which they have been seen – they are unmistakable.

Later on, on that memorable day we went together to Ghislaine's other studio where she keeps her larger work. As I was pulling out a particular canvas, clearly of museum quality, I turned to ask Ghislaine 'Can I have this one?' I could see my colleague frowning and the politest way to interpret his expression was . . . 'I think I brought Martin to see this work too soon!'

We went away, both completely overwhelmed by the impact of her work and we agreed that here was a very significant artist and that great care had to be taken to introduce her work to our respective clients. Would they see what we had seen? But we needn't have worried - her work has been selling within minutes of entering the gallery, giving the new owners great pleasure. Ghislaine's work has always been collected, but for her, selling has taken second place to producing and exhibiting, whether it be intimate works of herself and her family, landscapes or the large public commissions of various kinds that have established her critical reputation.

It was shortly after that first visit that I realised that Ghislaine needed a major book to herself and I was thrilled to find that her husband Michael was the author of the authoritative study on L.S. Lowry. It has been wonderful to watch my original idea of them working together develop from our first enthusiastic conversations into this beautiful publication. The book shows the extraordinary breadth, scope and emotional power of her work, and brings its special qualities to a wider public, giving them the opportunity to love and admire it as much as I do.

Introduction **Michael Howard**

This book is unusual, for it has been written as a dialogue, the two of us remembering our lives together, the ideas we've lived by and the things that have happened to us that have informed Ghislaine's work. So there are two independent voices, weaving together, sometimes as separate strands, but more often as a single unified thread. Though our roles are defined – mine as writer and hers as the maker – I hope that to some degree, we speak as one.

The book will seek out the roots of Ghislaine's paintings, her subject matter and style, her ambitions and achievements. We have tried to write the book with the forthrightness and honesty with which she approaches the craft of painting, and to document her struggle to create an accessible and ethical art in difficult times. Her sources are the rhythms of her daily life, either experienced directly, or by the secondary means of books, newspapers and the computer screen. Though steeped in the great patriarchal tradition of western art, she has always been conscious of painting as a woman and has worked hard to find her individual and authentic voice. We believe that the basic elements of human life are shared. What is art to do, if it is not to act as a constant reminder of this simple fact?

So this book has an agenda: it sets out to be critical and informative and to weave a narrative that will reveal the patterns that we now realise give Ghislaine's work a certain coherence and direction; something that can only be recognised in retrospect. Like the work of so many artists, Ghislaine's painting is essentially a private activity, even compulsive. The challenge for her is to make out of this highly personal activity, something that might act as a bridge between the artist, the viewer and the world, to enrich and inform experience. When asked to explain his art, Picasso once said simply, *'I am for life.'* This seems a suitable response. I hope that my relationship with Ghislaine and our shared lives together will echo Picasso's generosity of spirit.

Throughout the book Ghislaine is referred to by her first name; after all, I am her husband and it would be disingenuous of me to do otherwise.

Memory of our Wedding Day
2000
Acrylic on board
15.2 x 15.2 cm
Collection of the Artist

GHISLAINE HOWARD

A Biographical Sketch

However complex or difficult it might be to discern, any artist's work is inextricably bound up with his or her own life. And so a biographical account of the times in which Ghislaine has lived, the places and the people she has known, as well as the events that have touched her directly or indirectly, will serve to illuminate her art. An artist's original intention is often obscure, even to themselves, not only because paintings are created over a period of time, but also because the materials used have

a life of their own. Any painting is a complex interaction between the artist and the means by which she hopes to express her ambitions. Once finished, like children leaving the family home, paintings leave the studio to take on their own history. However difficult it may be

to articulate such concerns, it is a perpetual challenge to do so – a tantalising and seductive task for any artist and for those who seek out their work.

Early Years
Samuel Beckett once wrote that any conscious effort to recall the past 'provides an image as far removed from the real as the myth of our imagination or caricature furnished by direct perception'.[2]

Nevertheless, we can but try.

Ghislaine was born in Eccles, a town in Salford, part of the Greater Manchester conurbation. It is a town with a fascinating history, famous for its cakes, but also for having more pubs per head of population than any other town in England. Reputedly, it was in one of these, The Grapes in Church Street, that Friedrich Engels attempted to found the first communist cell, at the very time he was writing his world-changing book, *The Condition of the Working Class in England*.[3]

Ghislaine remembers the town as a thriving community, its streets lined with small shops clustered around a medieval parish church and the picturesque Victorian railway station that Lowry drew a number of times. Though so close to Salford, the town enjoyed a positive sense of its own identity, its terraced streets edged by industry and by the great Manchester

Ship Canal and the much smaller but no less historically important, Bridgewater Canal.

Though christened Ghislaine, her parents, Martin and Maureen Dobson, always called her by her middle name, Marianne. Martin was the son of a miner and grew up in the Northumbrian pit village of Cowpen (pronounced 'Coopen'). He left school at 14 and, fired by the ambition to become an actor, he gained a foothold in the Jesmond Playhouse in Newcastle upon Tyne, where many years later, Ghislaine would have her first one–person exhibition. Martin's career soon blossomed and he joined the Sheffield

Ghislaine's Father on Stage
Southport Little Theatre
1950

Harold Riley, Portrait of Ghislaine
1965
Pastel on paper
51 x 33 cm
Collection of the Artist

Bullfinch
c.1965
Ink and pastel
7.62 x 7.62 cm
Collection of the Artist

Repertory Company. In 1947, during a season at the Shakespeare Memorial Theatre, Stratford-upon-Avon, he met Maureen Ormonde who was working as a night sister at the Cottage Hospital in the town. From a once prosperous family, she had left a difficult home life in Ireland to find employment and a

new life in England. They fell in love and after a brief courtship, they married. It was a real *égoïsme à deux*. Martin was charismatic and charming – qualities that he kept and used to his advantage all his long life. Maureen was vivacious and unconventional, quick-witted and relentlessly funny and she immediately felt at home in this bohemian milieu. The theatrical world allowed them, in their own eyes at least, to rise above the constraints of class, lack of money and family background.

Ghislaine's elder brother Nicholas was born in 1948 and Ghislaine was born five years later, followed by Christopher in 1957, Michael

in 1960 and Adam in 1963. The financial insecurities of an actor's life took their toll and Martin reluctantly left the stage to take up a succession of jobs, one of which was collecting insurance premiums from the very streets that Lowry had known in his many years as a rent collector. In 1963 Martin set up an advertising hoardings company and Ghislaine remembers this period as a happy, though often unsettled, time; one fraught with anxiety, but redeemed by a strong sense

of family identity and home. She and her elder brother Nick found themselves taking on many domestic responsibilities, especially during the mid sixties when Martin and Maureen opened

and managed a short-lived but successful café/ restaurant in Eccles, with the engaging name, Polly Put.

Nothing ever remained stable in the Dobson household for long, as Martin and Maureen knocked down walls, built fireplaces, set windows in place and decorated and extended houses with scant regard for any issues concerning health and safety. Reproductions of works by Matisse and Gauguin kept company with paintings by Martin, together with Victorian prints and engravings bought at the local auctioneers, some of which still hang on our walls to this day. However, her father may not have been the greatest role model for a budding artist, as Ghislaine remembers:

Although a talented painter with a great feeling for paint, he always said that 'by the time you got out all your paints and set out your palette, all you really wanted was a cup of tea and 40 winks.

One of the most significant of Ghislaine's childhood memories was of being moved by a drawing of an old man seated by a dying fire, his head in his hands, consumed by grief.

At the sight of it, she burst into tears.

Vincent van Gogh, At Eternity's Gate ('Worn Out')
November 1882, The Hague
Lithograph
49 x 34 cm
Rijksmuseum Vincent van Gogh, Amsterdam

As the advertising business became increasingly successful, so the family found a certain stability, though Martin and Maureen could never bring themselves to trust their growing affluence and both of them suffered from an indefinable restlessness of spirit. Perhaps because of their backgrounds there was always a certain pressure within the family to achieve. Ghislaine's early love of drawing was encouraged, and the perceived need for her to succeed academically or otherwise was balanced by a recognition of this passion. From her earliest years, she drew obsessively on anything she could find – the back of old scripts, the end papers of books or the inside of Christmas or birthday cards, an activity she described as 'beeing' – a brilliantly apposite way to express the complete absorption that drawing can bring. As she grew older, she won several prizes for art including the Brooke Bond PG Tips Art Award. The prize was Adrian Hill's *What Shall We Draw?*, a book she still treasures to this day. One of the most significant of Ghislaine's childhood memories was of being moved to tears by a drawing on the back of a book. It was of an old man seated by a dying fire, his head in his hands, consumed by grief. At the sight of it, she burst into tears and when she asked her father about it, he replied that it was a drawing by van Gogh and that he was an artist who painted about feelings. A simple response that went straight to Ghislaine's heart, for from then on, she would ask when showing one of her drawings, 'Does it have feeling?'[4]

Her passion for art found expression in the drawing classes run by the Salford-based artist Harold Riley at the much-missed Buile Hill Park Museum. Harold was a great teacher, his enthusiasm was infectious and Ghislaine's confidence in drawing developed apace. She delighted in drawing the extensive collection of stuffed animals at the museum, which included an elephant, lions, monkeys and birds, many of which were arranged in dramatic tableaux to suggest movement, flight, or in the case of the lions, the struggle for survival itself. Harold encouraged her to enjoy the freedom of drawing with charcoal and pastel and Ghislaine began to discover the expressive possibilities of colour and texture – a revelation, as were the visits she made with her parents to his bohemian coach house and studio.

Her mother and father encouraged her emerging talent. Maureen had a tremendous eye for colour and Ghislaine's desire to be an artist was never seriously questioned. She remembers her father trying to arrange an exhibition of her work at the local library and being told to come back when she was grown up. Interestingly too, in the light of her subsequent history, Martin also wrote a letter to L. S. Lowry, in the hope that the great man might look at her work, but the request went unanswered.

Teenage Years

Ghislaine's teenage years were spent in an elegant detached Victorian house in Ellesmere Park, once lived in by George Bradshaw, the compiler of the first railway timetable. She attended Adelphi House Grammar School for Girls, a few hundred yards from Salford Art Gallery, then home to the Lowry collection. Her bus journey to school took her through the city, and past Oldfield Dwellings, one of the last remaining tenement blocks in Salford. Just around the corner from the school stood the elegant St Philip's church surrounded by the large Georgian houses of Encombe Place, all subjects drawn or painted by L. S. Lowry. The school, which was run by nuns, stood surrounded by industry on the banks of the River Irwell, its polluted waters running white with foam.

Michael
1999
Charcoal on paper
33 x 25.5 cm
Collection of the Artist

Art as it was taught in school was uninspiring, although her talent was recognised to a degree for Ghislaine recalls being accused of 'trying to be an artist before being a student' – a little notice box in fact, slapdash and careless. Her art teacher's passion was for architecture, and she took a very dim view of her pupil's propensity for self-expression. Ghislaine remembers terse remarks on her art homework, particularly: '6/10. Draw legs by Tuesday'. However, such memories are balanced by those of school outings to those parts of Derbyshire which she now knows as home, visiting medieval churches and the great houses of the region.

Ghislaine's mother had spent the happiest days of her difficult childhood with her aunt in the picturesque town of Birr in County Offaly, Ireland. In the mid sixties Martin and Maureen bought a run–down cottage on the outskirts of the town and from then on family holidays were spent there. These were idyllic times and until recently the family have kept a foothold in Ireland, and though that physical connection has now been lost, Ghislaine holds an Irish passport and continues to feel a deep connection with the place that she looks on as her second home.

In Eccles, she made lasting friendships that have remained great sources of strength and encouragement over the years. Debbie Horsfield, the playwright-to-be, lived in the house next door and she and Ghislaine became inseparable friends and later enjoyed student life together in Newcastle upon Tyne. A regular visitor to the family home was Tony Wilson, who was later to contribute so much to the Manchester cultural scene. He was a school friend of Ghislaine's brother Nick, and the two

would play guitar together, jamming the blues and the Rolling Stones. On occasion, Ghislaine would be encouraged to join in. She has very fond memories of Tony who remained a close friend of the family and became one of her first collectors.

Student Years

Ghislaine, still known by her middle name Marianne, applied for university and gained a place at the Fine Art department at Newcastle University. She had been well-prepared for her studies by a one-year Foundation course at what was then Manchester Polytechnic. She remembers her time there with great fondness and in particular the encouragement of her tutors, Melvyn Chantry, Don McKinley and Dave Pearson.

The creative freedom offered by the Foundation course was a revelation after the restrictions of school. She fully embraced the challenges of measured drawing, mark-making and discovered the expressive qualities of oil paint. She was introduced to printmaking, metal work and the idea of art as an experimental and dynamic practice without boundaries. And there was the undeniable thrill of being away from school and experiencing the excitement that going to Art College can bring.

Newcastle

The four-year course at Newcastle was something else. Studying there was made more significant to Ghislaine as she was to some extent returning home. Many of her relations lived in and around Blyth on the Northumbrian coast and were all known for their musicality and great, even eccentric, personalities. Things went well in the first

year; Ghislaine was a prize-winning student, producing a series of experimental and exciting projects in keeping with the aims of the first year programme. On entering the second year, however, her confidence began to falter and she found herself questioning her motivation, feeling the large abstract canvases that she had been working on over the summer were taking her in the wrong direction. She felt a need to get back to what had always mattered to her most, painting the figure. There followed a period of radical reassessment, emotional as much as artistic, which resulted in hundreds of works on paper, often of herself in her room or reworkings of mythological subjects.

It was obvious that the tutors were unsure how to cope with this change of direction and I was left very much to my own devices throughout the second year.

Nude on a Swing
(opposite)
1975
Oil on canvas
122 x 91.5 cm
Collection of the Artist

The Well-travelled Portfolio
Section of Ghislaine's University
portfolio

**Ghislaine at Manchester
University**
1972

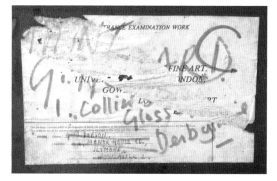

However, my developing relationship with Michael, with his deep feeling for, and knowledge of, art and literature gave me emotional security and reassurance throughout this period, when I was fraught with so many conflicting concerns, and opened so many new and often unexpected ideas for me to explore.

I had begun my studies with Ghislaine in the Fine Art department but I had gradually realised that my desire to be a serious painter would remain just that. And, though it is very odd to think about it now, I realise that I had always been convinced of Ghislaine's gifts, even though neither of us knew in what direction they would take her. We both shared a passion for literature and like so many of our generation, we devoured the Penguin Classics, and were entranced by their evocative covers. Together we read novels by Balzac, Flaubert, Zola, Hardy, Lawrence (*Women in Love* was a particular source of inspiration for Ghislaine), and many others. We enjoyed scouring the second-hand book shops of the city, competing with each other to find bargains and rarities,

always on the lookout for the beautiful art books published by Phaidon.

Meanwhile, I had applied and been accepted as a student on a new Art History course at the nearby polytechnic, now the University of Northumbria, just a stone's throw from the university. Encouraged by inspiring teachers, my way forward seemed clear, but for Ghislaine the question of how to make from her very personal works something that would be at once contemporary and accessible to others was a real challenge. And although the writings of Delacroix, Munch and Matisse helped, the answer, as always for Ghislaine, lay in work – work, work and more work.

Although I was still painting small oil studies, making etchings and countless drawings, I was prey to a thousand insecurities. This was a period of intense uncertainty for me, digging into my own world. I loved the immediacy and intimacy of direct drawing and painting, using tempera, painting directly onto unprimed canvas or paper. Maybe this was a way of building up my

confidence, testing the ground. I just couldn't find the necessary confidence to make the grand statements suggested by the very idea of painting oil on canvas. I don't know, but as I worked, things began to fall into place, and I found myself able to treat subjects that were obviously close to my heart and to take on the challenge of working in oils on a larger scale.

It was a rare piece of good fortune that this time coincided with a number of stunning exhibitions in Newcastle. Amongst these, was an exhibition at the University's Hatton Gallery that featured works of art from Glasgow's Burrell Collection which gave us time and opportunity to study a number of outstanding works at first hand – Gericault's *Leaping Horse* (c.1820) and Cézanne's magisterial *Chateau at Médan* (1882) were particularly important. There was an exhibition dedicated to Cézanne's drawings at the city's Laing Gallery, curated by Lawrence Gowing, a hugely significant event for us – to see Cézanne's creative energies at work, his struggles, clumsiness, even his downright

Salome
1973
Tempera on unprimed canvas
45.6 x 35.6 cm
Collection of the Artist

**Self-Portrait with Crouching
Venus**
1975
Oil on canvas
121.9 x 94 cm
Collection of the Artist

Mrs Miller
(Opposite) 1975
Oil on canvas
132 x 106.7 cm
Collection of the Artist

**Early Morning,
Belle-Ile-en-Mer**
1982
Acrylic on canvas
53.4 x 40.5 cm
Collect Art

Skull
1976
Etching and drypoint
15.2 x 15.2 cm
Private Collection

bloody-mindedness. Every one of these sublime works revealed how Cézanne moved from the sensual exuberance of his early years towards a humble openness before nature. Studying these drawings, we could see how each stage in this journey was schooled by an intense looking and a complete dedication to the task in hand – a life-changing experience.

During the Easter vacation in 1974, Ghislaine travelled to Paris with the university.

Strangely enough, the most profound impact came, not from paintings, but, as I now realise, from sculpture. I was hit by the physicality,

energy, movement and emotional power conveyed by the gestures of the Rodin sculptures at the Hôtel Biron and the two Michelangelo Slaves in the Louvre. These affirmed my ambition to express similar qualities in my own work. All of which prepared me for my meeting with the work of Edvard Munch in the winter of that year at the Hayward Gallery in London.

We remember that having spent far too much on prints at the exhibition, we had only enough money left for the coach to take us as far as Middlesbrough motorway service station. We arrived there late at night and were offered a lift to Newcastle from a kind lorry driver who

The Drowning
1976
Oil on canvas
180 x 122 cm
(Destroyed)

bought us the sweetest, sickliest hot chocolate we'd ever tasted. Ever since, the merest hint of hot chocolate operates as the madeleine dipped in tea did for Marcel Proust and we are sent right back to that memory.[5]

It was seeing this exhibition that took Ghislaine back into the life room with a renewed sense of purpose. We had both read and been excited by Munch's *Saint Cloud Manifesto* of 1889 in which he wrote, 'No longer shall I paint interiors with men reading and women knitting. I will paint living people who breathe and feel and suffer and love.' Munch's work confirmed what she had always felt; that the most important and significant art was that which reached across the barriers of time and place to touch our sensibilities – that had at its heart the primal sense of shared human experience: love, anxiety, sexuality, loss and the searching for one's place in the world. Munch's technical immediacy struck home too,

its directness and its urgency of expression. It posed difficult and pertinent questions – the danger of such ambitions and the delicate balance between pathos and the banal. This exhibition led Ghislaine to realise that ordinary life was itself extraordinary enough to serve as a starting point for such an art. With Munch she sensed that someone was expressing what she had always wanted to say without knowing exactly how.[6]

Ghislaine was excited by the immediacy of his attack, his innovative compositional structures and the emotional rawness of his figures that was tempered in other works by a great delicacy of touch and a sensitivity to the inner lives of his subjects. At times his work could be brutally crude, at others unerringly

subtle and compelling in its psychological underpinnings. We were also impressed by his unpitying self-regard and his understanding of art as a therapeutic, even obsessive, but never self-indulgent, activity. It could be vulgar too, and on occasion, clumsy and battered, but unforgettable.

It became evident that Ghislaine and I were attracted to art that stirred both the imagination and the intellect that, above all, would connect us with the very best that human beings can offer. This belief has not shifted, but only deepened over the years. We recognised then that, like music, the silent eloquence of painting and sculpture can transcend words and strike a resonant note deep within the human psyche. Munch's work, flawed though it may be, taught us that art need not be perfect, but that it is something made, *fait par la main*, and that this simple fact should not go unconcealed or uncelebrated.

Discophorus
(Top right) 1975
Oil on canvas
152.4 x 70.2 cm
(lost)

Discophorus
Silver gelatin print
Collection of the artist

'The criteria I use to judge to judge greatness in literary art is a work's power to break one's heart.'
John T. Irwin [7]

The impact of Munch's work was tempered by the diametrically opposed experience of seeing the restrained power and perfection of Renaissance art. In the summer vacation of 1974 we went to Italy for the first time and experienced together the shock of seeing in the original so many works we knew from reproduction. We travelled from Pisa to Florence, Bologna and then up to Mantua and across to Venice. The works that struck us most powerfully were the frescoes of Pisanello and Mantegna in Mantua, Tintoretto's *Pietà* in Milan and Titian's *Assumption* in San Rocco in Venice, and of course there were so many others. We were particularly moved and inspired by the contrast between the magnificence of Michelangelo's sculptures at the Accademia in Florence, and the quietude, elegance, simplicity and grace of Fra Angelico's frescoes in San Marco, Florence. There were so many other experiences of course, not all of

an artistic kind – nearly getting run over when we inadvertently slept out in a lovers' lane on the edge of Mantua, watching the sunrise from the Lido in Venice and the unforgettable taste of Italian coffee. These moments, all of them, have remained with us and continue to nourish Ghislaine's work, often in surprising and unexpected ways.

**Ghislaine,
Hotel Room, Paris**
1982
Photograph by Michael Howard

The life room was regarded at the time as something of an anachronism, a place where the traditional practice of measured, impersonal life drawing was still expected.

But for Ghislaine it was to become a battle ground.

**After Giovanni Bologna,
Samson Slaying a Philistine
[1560–2]**
1979
Graphite and wash on paper
18.4 x 14 cm
Collection of the Artist

On her return home she began a large self-portrait, which she worked on, completed, then scraped down and worked on again as she fought to resolve the demands that her experiences in Italy had provoked. The problem remained for her: how to capture the gravitas and humanity so evident in the works she had seen, especially when she felt herself so lacking in technical assurance.

Something else had also been set in place, perhaps unrecognised at the time – the added dimension of experiencing works of art in their original architectural settings. We relished the power of works still in those spaces for which they had been originally planned, hence our excitement at Fra Angelico's works at San Marco and the paintings of Tintoretto and Titian that glow in the shadowed glories of the Venetian and Florentine churches.

Such experiences were overwhelming and the third year was marked by a determination to find an appropriate response to the revelations of that summer. Ghislaine had always been struck by the silent presence of the numerous battered casts of antique sculptures that stood in the corridors of the university. Most of these were shrouded in dust, often with missing limbs and bearing the visible indignities laid upon them by generations of idle students. In a series of paintings and etchings she entered into a dialogue with those casts, with the life model and her own self-image. She was only too aware of the issues involved in such a course of study, for the life room was regarded at the time as something of an anachronism, a place where the traditional practice of measured, impersonal life drawing was still expected. But for Ghislaine it was to become a battleground.

I had the life model to myself, she was a powerfully built woman who approached the task of modelling with business-like efficiency. This was entirely fitting as her family and friends believed that she worked as a secretary at the university. I could paint and draw in the life room undisturbed for prolonged periods of time and work at my own pace through the concerns that, at times, almost overwhelmed me. Something that I found difficult to articulate in words, but I felt, at that time, that somehow the key to a proper and sustainable progress was here in the life room, and if I could get that key to turn, the door would open and I would be able to integrate my life and work, in the light of those artists that I admired and loved.

Our third year vacation was spent in Paris. We

were both writing dissertations on different aspects of Eugène Delacroix. We sat for hours at a time in the Chapelle des Anges in Saint Sulpice before his great fresco, *Jacob Wrestling with the Angel*, which he completed in 1861, shortly before his death two years later. Some of our happiest, most intense times were spent studying and copying that marvellous painting that, even then, unrestored, shone like a beacon from the murky depths of a cavernous and usually empty church. It was as important for us as it had been for those artists we admired, Degas (who once said, 'Delacroix, what a name for an artist'), Cézanne, Monet, Seurat, van Gogh and not least Matisse and Picasso, all of whom have paid homage in various ways to this great painting.

We stayed at the Hôtel de la Tournelle, a mock gothic monstrosity of a building that looked across the Seine to Notre-Dame. Nearby was the *Shakespeare and Company* bookshop. Our room was the very cheapest in that cheap hotel,

and appropriately enough it was a garret which we decorated with postcards and prints bought from *bouquinistes*, second-hand bookshops and galleries.

Ghislaine graduated in 1976, having worked in relative seclusion in the tower studio at the university with only a cast of the *Discophorus* for company. Her final show consisted of a number of powerful and highly ambitious works including a centrepiece – *The Drowning*. Like many of her works of this time, it has not survived.

After University

Ghislaine stayed on at Newcastle for a year teaching life drawing at the university whilst working towards a one–person show at the well-appointed gallery area connected to the Jesmond Playhouse theatre. We both remember some hair-raising moments as we carried her large canvases across a windswept Jesmond Dene Bridge. It was an uncanny experience, to have her first solo exhibition in the very place where her father had entered into the professional world of the theatre so many years before.

Exhibiting and selling a work in the Cleveland International Drawing Biennale of 1975–6 was

After Rodin, The Age of Bronze
(Above left) 1974
Ink and graphite on paper
12.7 x 14 cm
Collection of the Artist

Study after Delacroix, Jacob Wrestling with the Angel
(Above right) 1975
Oil on canvas
122 x 94 cm
Collection of the Artist

a significant moment – a major achievement in her own eyes and important in giving her the necessary confidence to accept a place at Goldsmiths' College of Art. We both looked forward to moving down to London, for I had achieved my ambition to study for an MA at the Courtauld Institute of Art.

London

We arrived in London in September 1977. I moved into university halls of residence in the centre of the city and Ghislaine found temporary accommodation living in the outer suburbs with an old school friend. Although we had been inseparable since our second year at Newcastle, in moving down to the capital together we both had realised that we were making a commitment to each other for life. This was something that we had never actually had to articulate to each other before – but cliché or not, actions speak louder than words.

Financial considerations meant that Ghislaine was unable to continue her studies at Goldsmiths, and although this was a disappointment to her, in some respects she had not felt completely at ease re-entering the enclosed world of the art school. The studios were set apart from the main college buildings and the whole experience seemed somehow retrogressive. And so she moved into a flat in Notting Hill Gate, a mile or so from where I was living, and found work in Fortnum & Mason's in Piccadilly, just across from the Royal Academy. It was draining to work the long hours, and galling to think of time passing and little painting being done. But the job had

its benefits too, such as meeting memorable characters, including the elderly Miss Mitchell who regaled Ghislaine with tales of her youth as a ladies' maid in a grand country house. She also remembers assisting Liberace as he tried on various women's hats. Such encounters gave her the opportunity to hone her powers of observation and memory, as she watched the modest dramas of buying and selling, and the interaction and gestures of shoppers and assistants alike – just as Degas had done a hundred years before. It was at this time that we began to see Degas for the great realist painter that he was – the true inheritor of all we had looked at so intensely as students. But such realisations were only a part of the general excitement of living in the capital, not as tourists or visitors, but as genuine inhabitants.

A little later we moved in together into a large ground floor bedsit on Russel Road in Kensington, overlooking the railway lines with Olympia in the distance. Our view from the window onto the street was enhanced by a beautiful flowering cherry tree. One corner of our room was dominated by an extraordinary non-functioning pink shower unit and large though it was, it still left space for a living area, a kitchen corner and workspace for Ghislaine and myself. The house was owned by the film director Michael Winner and was populated by a fascinating group of highly individual characters, actors, photographers and models, all trying to survive and find a foothold in their separate worlds. For the first time perhaps, we both felt totally accepted for what we were. It was a non-competitive community, the

very antithesis of a university department, and though gossip and intrigue were rife, there was a sense of genuine camaraderie, of unconditional friendship and support.

Ghislaine in particular, felt a tremendous sense of relief as we entered this new phase of our lives, for despite any shortage of money and the necessity of shop work, she felt that now in these new circumstances, she had a measure of emotional security. I was fully engaged in my academic life, the challenges and freedoms that it offered, and we were both immersed in the art, architecture and the thrill of being in London – a tremendous privilege.

In London, I found that I relaxed and opened up to the world. I produced work, modest work in the main, but work aimed to reconnect me with painting. I felt insecure in my craft and so the example of Matisse, the eternal student, was precious to me. I drew, painted, visited and revisited the galleries, especially the National Gallery and the Victoria and Albert Museum. But I was frustrated by a strange inability to paint the way I wished to. Small studies presented no problems, but larger work, that was something else – I felt constrained, uncertain, caught between so many possibilities, so many ambitions.

One of our greatest pleasures was attending evening life drawing classes supervised by Bunny, a very exacting teacher of the old school and a superbly gifted academic draughtswoman. We also enjoyed an extraordinary array of models, including one

who would talk all through the session to the artists for whom she had posed in her youth. She never appeared without full make-up and would welcome her imaginary guests into the room, conversing with them sotto voce throughout the session. Augustus John was a regular visitor, even though he had died in 1942. And then of course, there was the pub afterwards.

It was a transitional period in our lives, but also in Ghislaine's painting. A time of intense, intermittent frustration as ambitious works were blocked in with great verve, only to stutter and die under continual reworking; there were many beautiful studies and sketches, but as she remembers: *I was never satisfied. The paintings I admired were also silent reminders of all that I wished to achieve – the intensity and mastery I desired so much, but couldn't find.*

Such concerns were balanced by the constant availability of great works of art that were no longer a long and arduous journey away, but on our very doorstep. We drew continually, enjoying in particular Giovanni Bologna's *Samson Slaying a Philistine* (1560–2) at the Victoria and Albert Museum, the most mysterious of all museums perhaps, or so it seemed to us at the time. Ghislaine is still fascinated by the scarcely contained energy of these intertwining figures, with their spiralling forms and dynamic rhythms. She was also attracted by the Greek statues in the British Museum, never dreaming that one day she would exhibit there herself. Even now, this

Passerby, Russell Road
1979
Tempera and pastel on canvas
71 x 50.8 cm
Collection of the artist

realisation gives us a thrill. We studied the ever impressive Elgin Marbles, the colossal figure of Mausolus and the broken horse, a surviving fragment of the team that led his gigantic chariot group which topped the podium of the Mausoleum at Halicarnassus. We were also drawn to the Greek Tanagra figures, seduced entirely by their intimate self-containment, their grace and enigmatic beauty. Memories of the Durham Museum of Oriental Art drew us to the displays of Tang horses and Islamic ceramics, and these have remained constant sources of inspiration and delight.

London was still relatively deserted on Sundays and perfect for exploration by bike; we would visit Brompton Oratory to listen to the music and then cycle through the streets, squares and parks to Westminster Bridge, stopping at galleries as we wished. We loved our neighbourhood too; it was then a mixture of scruffy houses like our own and more affluent dwellings. We took delight in the old-fashioned charm of the nearby Lyons supermarket and teashop and the fascinating melange of antique shops of various kinds, the second-hand bookshops and vintage clothes shops. There was the excitement of the North End Road market and Earl's Court and through friends in the house, we became involved with the fringes of the theatre world, most memorably

perhaps, getting to know members of the cast and crew of the newly opened musical, *Evita*, which gave us access to a world of glamour and entertainment.

So many anecdotes, so many memories, there were a number of moneymaking enterprises too, such as making and selling handcrafted badges at Camden Market, each one painted with a different 'Miniature Masterpiece'. This was a source of great pleasure and invention, learning to paint with a directness, speed and surety as we copied the great masterpieces of western art and reduced each to the size of a matchbox.[8] Ghislaine also received her first portrait commission. This was from a wealthy Iranian, who had seen her easel in the window of our flat. Though he was happy with the result but nevertheless decided that the painting could be improved and his own status enhanced by the inclusion of a large Afghan Hound. This experience left its mark on Ghislaine, who to this day is still wary of accepting portrait commissions.

Return To Paris

It was a time when we could both enjoy the security of an established emotional life and we were able to take advantage of the benefits of my summer work in Paris. I worked for a company organising and directing the academic studies for visiting American students. I soon realised that there was more pleasure and education to be had travelling with the students across Europe than remaining in Paris. And so

it was that I, and occasionally Ghislaine, would spend the summer and Easter vacations on the road visiting the great towns and cities of Europe and earning money as I did so!

After finishing my MA, I gained a scholarship to study in France for a year to study the work of the French nineteenth-century artist, Théodore Chassériau. I spent most of my time in Paris, where I lived in an apartment that offered an iconic view of the Eiffel Tower that could almost have been a Delaunay painting come to life. Ghislaine and I divided our time between Paris and London, and once again, it was a privilege to experience a wonderful city, not as a tourist, but as a resident, if only for a year or so. We relished the silvery-blue light of Paris, the river with its bridges and slow-moving barges and knowing that Baudelaire and Balzac, Apollinaire, Matisse, Picasso and others had walked these streets was a continual encouragement to us both.

The example of Bonnard was significant to me, but it was not an easy time. I painted Passerby Russell Road, and the Pink Dress, intimate works, but I wanted something more. I desperately wanted to find a painterly equivalent for the totality of sensual experience that I found in Bonnard's work. These weren't just records of his own life, but documents of great understated emotional power. Michael was studying in Paris, and our conversations and visits to galleries together continued to inspire me to keep searching for a way to bring the separate strands of my life and art together.

We didn't only look at Bonnard of course;

there was an apparently endless stream of extraordinary works to be viewed and studied in Paris and elsewhere: the Avignon *Pietà*, the Botticelli mural, and above all, the paintings of Delacroix, the Impressionists and Picasso. Picasso's death in 1973 had profoundly affected us, but now in Paris his presence reasserted itself and showed us how art can survive death. It was an almost physical sensation – that what we understood to be important in the work of Picasso, Braque and Matisse was still possible and still relevant. Looking at paintings is like a love affair, some paintings connect and one knows from that moment that this one or that one will become constant companions; others perhaps, might prove to be more fickle, whilst others still might hide their light until a later date.

We will never forget the pleasures of exploring the book and print shops, one of which displayed a late Degas drawing of three dancers, not hanging on a wall, but set casually against some cabinets, next to an open door, as if the ladies were enjoying the breeze from the nearby River Seine. There was the excitement of buying Manet's small etching of the head of Baudelaire, and, a few weeks later, a Matisse linocut for 50 francs. Aside from art there were the pleasures of food and wine, sitting on the side of the river with bread and cheese, eating at the Petit Saint-Benoît, one of Picasso's favourite haunts, and at the nineteenth-century fast-food restaurant, Chartiers.[9] We travelled to Chartres, the Normandy coast and elsewhere, making some good friends and enjoying a very different kind of social life from the one we had in London.

Such experiences fed directly into Ghislaine's work and she began to feel confident enough

Memory of Aix-en-Provence
1980
Acrylic and pastel on canvas
30.5 x 63.5 cm
Collect Art

The Wedding: Ghislaine Dancing with her Father
(Opposite) 1981
Acrylic on canvas
53.3 x 45.7 cm
Collection of the Artist

Chinese Horse
Manchester Art Gallery
1984
Oil on linen
132 x 102.8 cm
Private collection

Paul Cézanne
The Diver
c.1867-70
122 x 94 cm
Amgueddfa Genedlaethol
Cymru
National Museum of Wales

to approach some London galleries to show her paintings. A number of opportunities presented themselves, but in the end she felt that she wasn't yet prepared for this step and so several opportunities were not taken up. This was a disconcerting and difficult time in terms of her painting and her ambitions, but in retrospect we both sensed that the moment for Ghislaine's art to come into its own still lay ahead.

Such positive and negative feelings were brought into focus as we continued our travels around Europe. Aside from France, we spent most of our time travelling in Italy where once more we were stunned by the gravitas of Cimabue's art (especially his *Crucifixion*, c.1265), Giotto and Masaccio. These works and countless others reinforced Ghislaine's desire to paint on a large scale and confirmed our understanding that paintings contain no single fixed meanings, but they can be many

things depending upon how and when they are seen. These encounters suggested that such works could be considered as a gift given by those now dead or absent to those living in the present who hold it in trust for those to come. This is a powerful idea and, for an artist and an art historian, it allows works of art to transcend the limitations imposed on art by a too narrow interpretation of history and chronology.

The religious content of those paintings we admired and their situations, often in the original church for which they had been intended, gave us food for thought. Although neither of us profess a religious faith, we do believe that at the heart of all religions is a connecting thread, one that embraces empathy, respect and understanding – and that these qualities, given shape in the teachings of the world's great spiritual leaders, are also shared by the best writers, poets, musicians and artists. All religious institutions are profoundly human

and few are untouched by barbarity, but how barren the world would be without the stories, art, music and the buildings connected with such ideas. And so we have always been particularly open to the ideas that underpin the Christian story and the fact that for better or worse, this is our heritage and one in which we find a welcome home.

As my studies at the Courtauld came to an end, I was offered a part-time job at the American University in Aix-en-Provence, and for a while it seemed as if we would live our lives in the shadow of Mont Sainte-Victoire and Cézanne, but when I was offered a full-time position at Manchester Polytechnic to teach in the History of Art and Design department, a tough decision had to be made. We made it and returned home to our native north-west, a decision that we both felt was the correct one. However much one might love the work of van Gogh, Cézanne, Matisse, the Fauves and Bonnard, we knew that essentially we were both northern creatures and that we would never be able to truly own the light and vivid colours of the south of France. We would always be tourists in Aix. Even then perhaps, Yeats's lines reminded us of the necessity of

Horses at San Marco
(Above) 2015
Graphite and watercolour on
paper
12.8 x 17.6 cm
Collect Art

Horse and Rider
2013
Oil on panel
22.8 x 30.5 cm
Collect Art

It's all well and good seeing works of art in books or on the computer screen, but nothing can equal an encounter with the real thing. The horses at San Marco, in Venice, once seen, can never be forgotten and Ghislaine has returned to them many times. These paintings are informed by her countless studies of horses from life, memory and imagination – as a young girl she dreamt of being a bare-back rider in a circus.

She had time to paint, but now the pressures of what to paint
and how to paint it remained uppermost in her mind.

returning 'to where all ladders start, to the foul rag and bone shop of the heart'. It was the right choice, although at the time we were very unsure how this momentous decision would affect us.

The Return To Manchester & The First Exhibitions

As a native of Liverpool, it was a strange experience to find myself living and working in our rival city of Manchester, but for Ghislaine it meant a return to her roots. For both of us, the unexpected security of my finding a permanent position at the Art School was a novel experience. We lived in a small terraced house on Canal Bank, Monton, and from her studio window Ghislaine could look out over the bright orange waters of the Bridgewater Canal, its colour caused by the water passing through earth rich in iron oxide. On the opposite bank stood a large red-brick mill such as Lowry used to paint and a little further along was a tripe works. It was a fascinating place to live, full of incident. Ghislaine was now able to dedicate herself to painting full-time and was excited by the challenge of making her unexpected return a positive force in her work. The experience of living in London and travelling abroad enabled her to look at her once familiar environment in a new light. As

a painter, Ghislaine has always been led by her practice and as we look back, it seems evident that her artistic ambitions only really fell into place when she came back home: resistance and acceptance.

We married in October 1980, in Saint Mary's church, Eccles, a large ugly red-brick Victorian structure, replete with nineteenth-century Italian sculptures and the gaudily painted *Stations of the Cross* which had fascinated Ghislaine as a child. The wedding was a joyful, informal occasion, people travelled from London and elsewhere, and afterwards Ghislaine painted some intimate remembrances of the day, relishing the exuberant splendour of the pink and white frills that lined the marquee. Our honeymoon was spent in the unlikely destination of Newbiggin-by-the-Sea in Northumberland, where Ghislaine had spent many childhood holidays, and a place that we had visited many times together as students.

It was a great pleasure to create a domestic space that was ours, and ours alone. We developed the small garden area at the front of the house and enlivened the backyard with a few flowerbeds. We found ourselves living in a close-knit community of characterful neighbours, all of whom it seemed knew each other's business and were always ready to give advice on

any number of issues, including Ghislaine's painting. Everywhere we looked there was evidence of industrial decline: buildings that had once seemed so permanent to Ghislaine were now empty, falling into ruin or awaiting demolition and just beyond the town the once busy industrial areas were slipping slowly into dissolution. Walking towards Manchester along the canal, we would pass row upon row of terraced houses shadowed by the imposing structures of mills and factories – some still in use, but most now empty or home to countless small businesses of various kinds. Following the towpath in the other direction, it was easy to fall into the illusion of being in open country with fields and woods on either side, only to have that illusion shattered by the shock of coming across the massive concrete presence of the M60 cutting through the once extensive acreage of Worsley Woods. A little further afield lay Barton, Pendlebury and Trafford Park, then a veritable *terrain vague*. Until the late nineteenth century it had been the home of the de Trafford family until it became the first planned industrial estate in the world. It remains the largest in Europe but by this time industry had virtually disappeared from the park – a poignant reminder of a lost world and the workers who inhabited it. Adjacent to this man-made wasteland was an eerie collection

of lanes, fields and semi-derelict farms, one of which sold free-range eggs amidst a collection of broken-down lorries, farm machinery and ruined cars. With the destruction of the physical and material aspect of Salford and Eccles, something was lost of its soul. Small wonder then our minds went back to Lowry and we began to seriously think about him. Ghislaine was determined not to become one of his clones, but she could not escape the attraction of painting such scenes, learning as much from the example of Sickert and Whistler as from the paintings of Valette and Lowry.[10]

Abutting Salford was the urban sprawl of Manchester itself with its Victorian and Edwardian architecture, museums and art galleries. The blunt presentness of the two cities acted as a catalyst and enforced the apparent necessity, for Ghislaine, of repossessing her northern sensibility. She had time to paint, but now the pressures of what to paint and how to paint it remained uppermost in her mind. In retrospect, the solution seems obvious, but it

was less so at the time: like Degas, you paint your surroundings, yourself, your friends and family and avoid anecdote, sentimentality and any temptation to deviate from a firm faith in what art can and should do.

The Monks Hall Show, 1982

Ghislaine was beginning to work in a consistent and focused way and, as she had hoped, the various strands of her life and art were now beginning to weave together into a consistent working practice. She made paintings of the domestic scene, memories of our recent wedding, our travels and her response to

Ghislaine Preparing for her Exhibition at Monks Hall Museum
Eccles Journal
1982

View from the Studio Canal Bank, Monton
1981
Oil on board
40.7 x 30.5 cm
Collection of the Artist

Ghislaine has her preferred colours and certain favoured juxtapositions, indian reds against ultramarine, for example, or Naples yellow against cerulean blue.

But her decisions are always intuitive.

Maureen in the Yellow Kitchen
1982
Acrylic and pastel on canvas
63.5 x 81 cm
Private collection

her new surroundings, such as *The Yellow Kitchen*, which, though painted in our house at Monton, seems filled with Mediterranean light. There were demolition scenes, millscapes and images of local people, such as *Going Home in the Snow* which, looking back, seems to be an unconscious acknowledgement of Lowry's achievement. Lowry was becoming for us something more than the cardboard cut-out promoted by the media. She recorded and celebrated our holidays in Normandy, Brittany and our visits to Ireland and painted our new

friends and her old childhood friends – albeit with a greater power and conviction than before. Ghislaine was learning much from looking evermore closely at the works of Vuillard and Bonnard, and studying their intimate evocations of space, light, atmosphere and their emotional and suggestive powers. She also envied their technical virtuosity. From their example and that of Degas, Ghislaine developed a distinctive use of monotype, spreading ink thinly over a glass plate, laying

down a piece of paper and drawing into it, allowing the ink from the glass to impress itself upon the paper. This gave an almost lithographic quality to the resulting print. These images have a striking intimacy, sometimes the monotypes were left in their original state, and sometimes, like Degas, she would enrich them with an overlay of pastel.

Ghislaine applied to Salford Art Gallery and was offered a show at Monks Hall Museum in Eccles.[11] It was a modest venue, but a significant one. Ghislaine had known it since childhood and one of Lowry's most important exhibitions had taken place there. Many Salford artists have exhibited there over the years, including Geoffrey Key and Harold Riley. To publicise the exhibition, Ghislaine made a screen print from a drawing she had made whilst holidaying at Pont-Aven earlier in the year.

One of our fondest memories of Canal Bank was the response of our neighbour, Dorothy, a formidable local character, who, on seeing us carrying out one of Ghislaine's large still lifes to the car in readiness for the exhibition, called out to her husband, 'Here, Terry, come out and look at this, now that's real art!' Dorothy's unsolicited response was like an unofficial blessing on what was, for Ghislaine, a momentous occasion – her first exhibition in her home town. The exhibition gave Ghislaine the necessary impetus to seek out a gallery in Manchester and soon she began to show work with the artist and dealer, Colin Jellicoe, whose small city centre gallery on Portland Street has been a Manchester institution for over 40 years. He had introduced her to Tony

Gordon, at the Portland Gallery and who later curated a highly successful series of jewellery exhibitions. Colin showed Ghislaine's work at the Edinburgh Festival in 1983 which in turn led to a relationship developing with the Flying Colours Gallery in that city. The advice, encouragement and support given by both Colin and Tony in these early years of Ghislaine's career cannot be overestimated.

The Royal Exchange Exhibition

Earlier that year, Ghislaine had shown a group of related works entitled *Images of Women* in the exhibition space at the Royal Exchange Theatre, Manchester. This was a significant event – there were good sales and some happy memories, not least the response of one visitor to her *Self-Portrait Torso*, who presumably deeply moved by the work's tactile qualities was spotted covertly caressing the canvas. Other paintings in the show revealed Ghislaine's delight in the processes of picture-making. Her subjects were her friends and her immediate world, the results lyrical and decorative, strong compositions that avoided any sense of prettiness or the picturesque for its own sake.

The exhibition revealed what would become a defining aspect of Ghislaine's future shows; although each painting was complete in itself, each one also played its part to create an overall mood or atmosphere. The paintings seen together showed women, alone or in groups, interacting in public and private spaces. The realisation that this was the case encouraged her to become more sensitive to the impact of social spaces on her subjects. Ghislaine has

Michael in the Bath
1984
Acrylic on canvas
61 x 101.6 cm
Collection of the Artist

never been a theory-based artist, but rather she has always focused upon a few key ideas. Two such ideas began to grow in significance in Ghislaine's thinking – the nature of public and private spaces and the image of the body in movement – and of course, no one handled those issues better than Degas. His art and his many aphorisms remind us that movement is the key to life itself: 'It is the movement of people and things that consoles us. If the leaves on the trees didn't move, how sad the trees would be — and so should we!'

In 1984 Ghislaine was offered a major one–person exhibition at Salford Art Gallery. Important as such exhibitions are, equally important is the support offered by the commercial sector. Sales and encouragement from the private galleries fuelled her other more ambitious, less immediately saleable works. She began to show at the Pitcairn Gallery (later Wendy Levy Fine Art) in Knutsford and with Agi Katz at the Boundary Gallery, in London. She came to the attention of the curator John Sheeran, who included her in an exhibition dedicated to the Yorkshire landscape in Leeds.

There was also a fruitful relationship with the *British Medical Journal*, and the Galerie Horizons in Brussels. In Manchester, Ghislaine exhibited with Jan Green at the Tib Lane Gallery. Jan was the doyenne of Manchester art dealers and dealt with the work of artists both she and we admired: painterly painters such as Sickert, Lowry and Joseph Herman.[12] She also had an evangelical zeal for the sensitive oil sketches of Adolphe Valette and regularly showed gouaches and drawings by Keith Vaughan, and one of these still hangs on our bedroom wall. Jan became Ghislaine's major dealer, but also showed my work and later that of our daughter, Cordelia. Both of us were involved in Manchester's cultural life; I gave talks in the city and Ghislaine showed work at the Castlefield Gallery, founded in 1984, by a group of ex-students from the Art School.

During these years I was offered various opportunities to lecture around the UK and in London. For many years I was a regular contributor to the Modern Art Studies course, then based at the Institute of Contemporary Arts in London, and then later at Christie's

Education. Through these activities, in1998 I met Cynthia Corbett who, on seeing Ghislaine's work, offered her the opening exhibition at her new London gallery and the two became firm friends. Cynthia still remains Ghislaine's London gallerist and has collaborated with her on numerous projects in London and elsewhere.

The Salford Show

of 1985 was a landmark event for Ghislaine. She received much encouragement from the curators at Salford, in particular, Neil Wilkie, whose passion for ceramics and glass resulted in a number of paintings of the gallery that complemented those she was producing, inspired by the ceramics and paintings in Manchester Art Gallery. As Ghislaine was expecting our first child, there was some question as to whether or not she should postpone the exhibition. However, she was unwilling to do this and the exhibition went ahead as planned with Ghislaine not only completing the work for the show, but also constructing the frames. The exhibition

Pregnant Self-Portrait
July 1984
Oil on board
78.8 x 58.5 cm
Collection of the Artist

Family Life: The First Pregnancy

Journeys abroad were still an essential part of our lives. We remember some of these moments with exceptional vividness as life-changing encounters. Duccio's *Maestà*, his monumental double-sided altarpiece completed in 1311, for example. We were prepared for the sheer singing beauty of Duccio's work, but our meeting with the actual object was something else – and maybe even then, the idea of a series of small paintings entered Ghislaine's mind. In Monterchi, we saw for the first time Piero della Francesca's fresco of the *Madonna del Parto*, (1460) – a revelation.[14] Ghislaine was pregnant herself, and it was a moving experience to see her, standing before it, in a deep blue tunic dress, looked down upon by Piero's serene, imperious and unutterably beautiful pregnant Madonna. Our memory of this occasion has merged with Michael Ayrton's moving essay of 1960 about his own pilgrimage to the same painting.[15] Echoes of Piero's Madonna can be felt in many of Ghislaine's later works, not least in the 25–foot high Liverpool Hope University altarpiece, the *Visitation*, that she completed in 2002.

In the months immediately preceding the show and several months before Max was born, we had moved into a flat in Ghislaine's childhood home, the large Victorian detached property

featured such paintings as *Chinese Horse, Manchester Art Gallery* a sequence of pregnant self-portraits, a number of mother and child, and father and child paintings and such works as *Michael in the Bath*. Parenthood had made it very clear to Ghislaine that as a woman she now had the occasion to paint not just maternal themes so common in western art, but to revisit that tradition by painting domestic life from her own point of view.

The critic and academic Jim Aulich wrote in *City Life* that 'Ghislaine Howard's recent work shows the dignity of the human being and an almost French sensuality in the love and freedom of paint. Domestic and intimate subject matter tells of the artist's pregnancy, and the birth and suckling of her child, while in the bath lies the image of a man in a self-conscious inversion of Bonnard's theme of the woman in the bath. Luscious and unorthodox, these pictures are strikingly original in what they depict within the context of the museum and the tradition of figure painting.'[13]

Max, 'Feet to the Stars'
1990
Conté pencil on Ingres paper
15.2 x 22.8 cm
Collection of the Artist

set amongst the tree-lined roads of Ellesmere Park in Eccles. We lived on the ground floor with her former attic bedroom now operating as her studio. It was here, as her pregnancy became more evident, that she began to chart in an intuitive manner the psychological and physical changes of her own being.

As a painter whose work springs from my own experience, my pregnancy presented a challenge that I could not ignore without denying the central basis of my inspiration. This challenge was the pictorial representation of the pregnant figure and to record and interpret my own pregnancy and subsequent motherhood.

Her condition allowed her to realise that rather than striving for something 'out there', all that was important was ready to hand. It was at this juncture that her mother's friend, a former midwife, visiting the studio, saw the painting, *Pregnant Self-Portrait, July 1984*, and said in conversation, 'I know just how that feels.' The statement struck an immediate chord with Ghislaine and reminded her of her father's comment about the van Gogh drawing that had struck her so forcibly as a child. What are the implications of that phrase, 'just how that feels'? It suggests not just the delights of approaching motherhood, but the attendant anxieties as well.

I remember being caught up with an enveloping sense of introspection and the growing realisation that my life was about to change forever. Such feelings coexisted with the novel sensation of my body being taken over by something or somebody else. Such thoughts and emotions coloured almost

every aspect of those months and weeks before the expected date of Max's birth.

This spontaneous remark hit home and quickened Ghislaine's resolve to paint not just the look of things, but as van Gogh and others have made evident, how things 'feel', and in so doing, to make sense of a momentous and entirely personal experience. She watched the shape of her body change and became sensitive to shifts in her persona too, as she became increasingly aware of the experience to come. An experience Sylvia Plath described vividly in her poem 'Metaphors': that having 'boarded the train there's no getting off'. Amongst all these tumultuous feelings, another made itself known: a realisation that the excitement and

anxiety of being pregnant and giving birth had parallels with painting itself – both had at their very centre the thrill of bringing something new into the world.

Parenthood – Max is Born

However, any plans that Ghislaine had in mind to develop her drawings and studies into a sequence of major canvases were curtailed when life interrupted art. Max was born a month early on 28 August 1984. Weighing only four pounds and severely jaundiced, he had to be taken into the Special Care Baby Unit where he was kept under observation for two weeks. This was a traumatic time for us both and particularly for Ghislaine, although the inevitable feeling of helplessness

was partially assuaged by being able to sketch him in his incubator. Max responded well to treatment and I waited with great anticipation for the homecoming of them both, preparing the flat for the new arrival. But when Ghislaine came home, the initial elation she felt soon evaporated and she was hit by an unexpected sense of anxiety and depression which lasted for some time. Eventually it passed as the joy of having Max asserted itself and she once again began to draw and make studies of our new domestic situation. These feelings were accentuated as the drawings and studies of Max accumulated.

Ghislaine became entirely absorbed in every aspect of Max's life, watching his rapidly developing communication skills, his growing strength and burgeoning personality, and her drawings and paintings clearly reflect her (and my) ever-deepening love for him. None of this was done in a documentary spirit, far from it. The motivating agency was the realisation that these precious moments were passing by so quickly and that as an artist, Ghislaine had the means to hold onto the memories and significance of each stage of Max's young life. Like many parents, she found joy and inspiration in the everyday moments of family

Michael and Max, Contre-jour
1984
Oil on canvas
182.9 x 91.4 cm
Collection of the Artist

None of this was done in a documentary spirit, far from it.

routine, washing, dressing, eating and so on. Through painting, something of these fleeting moments could be held for ever. Allied to this was the ambition to make such works, formed by deeply personal experiences, ones that could reach beyond the personal to touch others. This desire to connect not only with the viewer, but also with artists of past, is a characteristic that is a constant in Ghislaine's mind – to revisit, reaffirm and reinvent traditional imagery. Suddenly the well-worn motif of the mother and child becomes not a cliché, but something personal and urgent that demands expression as a marker of shared human experience.

In such images as *Mother and Child: Self-Portrait with Max*, we see the ambivalence of a child's response to a mother's loving embrace. Max is caught in mid-movement, half accepting, half pulling away. Such paintings record any child's growing need for independence and the parent's corresponding desire to hold onto every precious moment with their child. A painter's task is to find a means through paint and line to evoke such feelings without slipping into easy sentiment or the anecdotal, but to suggest something of the gravity, affection and melancholy of such moments. Why melancholy? Simply because as the many paintings of the Madonna and Child suggest, time moves on and things will come to pass as they will.

On a personal level, we were very aware that we had moved from a simple relationship of two individuals to a family unit – becoming parents made us realise that our own parents were now grandparents. An obvious point perhaps, but one that gave Ghislaine a renewed sense of the chain of being – and together with her hospital experience provided fresh impetus to her desire to chart the experiences of the everyday. As Max moved from babyhood to infancy, Ghislaine, like the poet, Sylvia Plath and so many others, watched herself become increasingly absorbed in her baby's development. Day by day, growing evermore fascinated by the independent being of her child, the power and mystery of the processes that Plath describes so well in her poem, You're:

Clownlike, happiest on your hands,
Feet to the stars...[16]

These experiences reinforced Ghislaine's sense of kinship with the great painters of the past, Titian and Rembrandt, Cézanne and Degas, all artists who could endow the visual with a sense of the communicating touch. As we look at such artists' work we register the play of line and colour, an interaction that gives life to the painted forms and allows them to breathe and brings the viewer into the creative experience. So it was exhilarating for both us to find that my life with Max became a central theme in Ghislaine's work; there are so many images of mothers with their children in art, and so few of fathers interacting with theirs. The 1980s and 1990s were decades in which the traditional views on pregnancy and childbirth were being questioned by academics, artists, writers and health professionals as well as by mothers and mothers-to-be themselves. Ghislaine was no different; without thinking in such terms or being consciously aware of the debate, from 1984 pregnancy and motherhood became a major theme in her art. Although there were a number of artists of the time dealing with subjects that echoed Ghislaine concerns, they did so in a fashion

Michael Reading Rupert to Max
1987
Oil on canvas
91.4 x 91.4 cm
Collection of the Artist

Drinking Tea with Max
1984
Charcoal on paper
76.2 x 55.9 cm
Collection of the Artist

life; separation, the moment the child begins to have an awareness of their own being as an independent entity. After all, we teach children to walk partly in order that one day they will be able to leave the family home.

Looking

Surprisingly perhaps, D. H. Lawrence's essays on his own paintings and those of Cézanne catches something of this as do the writings of Avigdor Arikha.[17] Lawrence's 'Introduction to These Paintings', first published in 1929, promotes with an infectious enthusiasm the need for an art that is direct and visceral. An art that should not just describe, but that should hit the viewer directly with the force of what it is to look, to really look at the world in a way that we rarely do. The world is not as a photograph might suggest, unchanging with clean edges; it is the exact opposite, contingent, dynamic, ever-shifting and uncertain, but marvellous in its ambiguities. Ghislaine celebrates such nuances. Her works have a convincing solidity, but her forms are left open, and the boundaries are blurred to suggest movement of bodies within space and time. Lawrence does not forget to remind his reader how the materiality of the body connects with the materiality of paint. A powerful and resonant idea, especially for an artist like Ghislaine for whom the body signifies the totality of the physical self: the

that Ghislaine instinctively and intellectually could not embrace. Instead she found nurture in the fierceness of the love that Käthe Kollwitz (1867–1945), had for her sons and, above all the equally fierce love shown in Berthe Morisot's paintings of her daughter, Julie. Morisot (1841–95), was possibly the first modern artist who painted women's experiences from a woman's point of view. She painted with an improvisatory technique very much akin to Ghislaine's own. She focuses in on the point of maximum interest, allowing the rapidly placed brushstrokes to weave into a loose network of colour that becomes denser and more telling as the point of major interest is reached, pictured and fully described. It is

a way of painting that depends upon selective focus – at once animating the subject and enmeshing it in a field of energy. And so Ghislaine began to value more and more those artists who looked and worked with an intensity of vision, who give the viewer a sense of discovery and empathy, engaging with what we might call the tactility of vision. In such paintings, the viewer can almost relive, touch even, the things drawn and painted but also feel something of the creative energies expended in the creating of that image.

The paintings of this time are sensitive to two opposing energies: that of communion and separation. Communion in the paintings of pregnancy and the very first months of a child's

At the Easel with Cordelia
1987
Acrylic on board
36x24

Suddenly the well-worn motif of the mother and child becomes not a cliché, but something personal and urgent that demands expression as a marker of shared human experience.

mind, imagination, memory, hand and eye working together as the place from which the artist 'speaks'.

As a painter I have to be wary of overthinking, of deliberately seeking out theoretical justifications for my work, but it is fascinating to consider where an artist's ideas originate. I would much rather that any such concerns should become part of my practice without my realising it consciously. I think that this is very important – never to let concepts rule, but to remain open to anything that life brings along. But such thoughts go hand in hand with the deep pleasure and excitement that I felt, and continue to experience, as Michael discusses with me his latest ideas, book projects or forthcoming lectures. And as I began to take on some occasional teaching myself and to give talks about my work, so I became increasingly sensitive to the ideas that inform and attempt to explain our contemporary situation.

Ghislaine goes to great lengths not to emulate any superficial stylistic qualities of those artists that she admires, but takes to heart their deep practice, their inner drive and dedication. For

her, like many artists, painting the landscape is a way of allowing her ideas – technical, emotional and intellectual – to find expression in paint without the many challenges associated with painting the figure. Our travels and the paintings that result have helped to suggest to her the best ways of finding a pictorial equivalent to the shock of experience. To carry back what has been learnt in the field, into the studio. We particularly remember being astounded by the colour and expansiveness of the Scottish landscape for example, which we remember unfolding before us as we listened to Wagner's *Ring Cycle* on our car's sound system. Equally important are the memories of family holidays in France and Italy – the cliffs at Normandy, Pourville, Etretat and Houlgate which we appreciated not least for their associations with Monet. It was also for myself a landscape redolent of all that I loved in the late work of Braque and the writings of Proust. All these experiences, reading and seeing,

thinking and doing, feed back into the melting pot of Ghislaine's imaginative and creative practice.

Friends and Family Life

We were fortunate in making some great friends, including the art historian and painter Richard Kendall with whom I shared an office at the School of Art (Polytechnic), as well as Richard and Belinda Thomson, also art historians, whose knowledge of, and dedication to, their subject is a byword in my field of study.

Richard Kendall was not only an exceptional teacher and colleague, but also a perceptive

critic with an acute visual intelligence, who was beginning at that time to move away from teaching towards a career in writing and curating that would eventually take him to the USA. At this time however, he lived in the village of Broadbottom on the Cheshire / Derbyshire border. Once a valley dominated by mills and industry, it is now a picturesque commuter village for Manchester, with spectacular views and rows of charming stone-built houses. We fell in love with the area and were excited when one of Ghislaine's oldest friends who lived in the nearby town of Glossop told us of an extraordinary property that had just come on the market – a former tripe works in the centre of town. It was situated at the lower end of a steep street of terraced houses, looking out from a height over the town hall and market place. One of its main features was a large windowed front room that had originally been a shop. Behind this were the living quarters which in turn led to the tripe

works itself. That part of the property, still with its machinery intact, perched precariously on the steep banks of Glossop Brook facing what was once the largest textile mill in Europe. Now a hotel, its sandstone facade rises like a gigantic cliff face above the intervening brook. A ginnel led from the street to a cobbled courtyard which gave access to what is now a terraced garden, but was then nothing but a collection of broken-down bits of outbuilding which dropped down towards the brook, some 60 feet below. From here one could look out down the valley, an unimpeded view that opened out to the hills. In the distance, the Snake Pass that traverses 24 miles of open moorland before reaching Sheffield; a magical place. We managed to acquire the property and set to work with a will to make it suitable for our purposes. Thirty years on – we're still working on it.

The Garden, Glossop
1987
Oil on canvas
101.6 x 50.8 cm
Collection of the Artist

Shadow and the Geese
1997
Watercolour on paper
17.8 x 20.4 cm
Private collection

Michael Walking with Shadow: Homage to L.S.L.
(Opposite) 1999
Acrylic on board
15.2 x 15.2 cm
Collection of the Artist

> Ghislaine tore the paper, letting it fall onto the studio floor, only to have our dog Tess come running in from the garden, straight across the paper, leaving her muddy paw prints as evidence of her intervention.

I think that we both instinctively noticed the building's potential as a theatrical, even mythical place, a place that would help us both fulfil our needs. I remember coming down one morning, shortly after we had moved in, and seeing my father, who had come to visit, sitting at the garden's edge, a mug of tea in hand. Below him, the brook that would eventually join the Mersey, where he had worked as a customs officer in Liverpool for so many years. He didn't notice me, and I didn't say anything. He died not long afterwards. Of all the memories I have of my father, that one is the most precious.

Ghislaine immediately took over the former shop area at the front of the house as a studio, and Max, and later Cordelia, grew up in a house that was permanently being altered according to our needs, Ghislaine's family history repeating itself perhaps? But both children, from their earliest years seemed to have an innate understanding of the nature of Ghislaine's art and her professional needs.

Having my studio in the house was crucial. When the children were small I only had a few child-free hours a week, so working time had to be taken whenever it could. Fortunately, Max had an extraordinarily rich imaginative life and so he would happily spend hours playing quietly, drawing, looking at books, or watching television (thank God for Sesame Street and Tintin!), whilst I painted, and of course he was always a ready and, I like to think, willing model.

Our feelings about the house and garden during this period are beautifully expressed by a poem that Max wrote when he was about ten years old.

My Kingdom

I am a king within my kingdom
Gold streams through my walls
My servants are devoted and from them silver falls.
My boundaries are marked out with plants and eiderdown,
These all let strangers know my kingdom from the town,
But prowling round my kingdom vicious monsters roar;
They terrorise my servants with sharpened tooth and claw.

My gold is the sunlight,
My servants the geese
My kingdom a green field
My dogs the beasts.

Glossop lies sheltered in a valley at the foot of the Pennines that leads out to the windswept moors and broken edges of the Dark Peak. It is surrounded on three sides by the sculpted hills and crags of Bleaklow to the north-east whilst the plateau of Kinder Scout rises to the south. The town itself is overlooked by the folded forms of the mysterious Whitley Nab. In Pigot's *Commercial Directory of Derbyshire*, 1828-9, the town and its surroundings are described thus: 'The country round here is very pleasing, and many of the views are romantic, enriched by plantations, which abound in the home scenery. The lands on the low grounds are fertile, but the mountainous parts are less productive.' A description that still rings true despite the encroachment of modern times.

It is a landscape frequently shrouded by low-lying cloud which, if the sun is shining, can trap the light between the often damp streets and the floor of the clouds above to create the very special quality of light that Lowry loved and made his own. And though we didn't know it at the time, it was here that the young Geoffrey Key came to find his voice as a painter in the mid seventies. For myself, there was the intense excitement of learning that a few miles south of the town on Chunal Moor, the philosopher Wittgenstein had lived and worked as a young student at the Grouse Inn in the early years of the last century, making large

The Moors at Chunal
1987
Ink and watercolour on paper
25.4 x 50.8 cm
Collection of the Artist

Our daughter Cordelia was born on 20 July 1987. Being pregnant for the second time, Ghislaine realised that if she wanted to record this experience, she would have to do so with a certain amount of urgency, and a whole series of studies and self-portraits followed. Previously, Ghislaine had been content to show herself clothed, but this time the work is marked by a more confrontational gaze – often she depicted herself naked looking at her own reflection in the studio, bedroom or bathroom mirrors. Her earlier pregnancy drawings and paintings had shown a certain introspective mood, but these works reveal a more frank appraisal of the changes she was undergoing. Her work generally was gaining a bolder and freer approach as may be seen in her 1995 *Saskia Pregnant*, painted over a single day for a television film. There was also of course the shared pleasure that she found in painting our friends, their pregnancies and their babies, particularly Christine Waygood and Jane Matthews.

Cody kites for students from the university who would use them to run experiments in the upper atmosphere. We have enjoyed walking the moors with our friends, especially Alastair Noble, whom I have known since childhood, retracing the footsteps of the young Wittgenstein, and like him, sending our kites high into the clouds. Ghislaine gave Alastair a small watercolour that hangs in his New York apartment. In a letter to us, Alastair described it thus: 'Looking at it in the warmth of my apartment, I am immediately transported back to the landscape above Chunal. It catches the tempestuous elements of the moors exactly; those sudden shifts in the weather that can take you by surprise and I'm captivated by that tiny spot of light that shines in the heart of darkness.'

It is one of the great delights of being a painter that one can give and receive such gifts.

It is an abiding pleasure to live in close proximity to the changing forces that shape our environment, the weather, the seasons and the time of day. But, above all, it is the emptiness and the unpredictability of this great landscape that attracts us – its textures, folds and colours, its brooding presence that lies at the opposite end of the spectrum to the picturesque.

Primarily a painter of the figure, Ghislaine finds painting the landscape an exhilarating practice and though she may work from sketches or photographs, her preference is to paint in front of her chosen motif, in this manner she is able to respond to the immediacy of the situation with a corresponding speed and directness of action; to allow the promiscuous interaction of colour and line find an equivalency for the force of a river pouring from its source down a hillside, or the clouds obscuring or revealing the splendours of form and void, stillness and movement. This practice allows paint to sing as paint – to give it a life of its own, responding to the very energies she seeks to capture, energies that cut through the superficial aspects of appearance to express what lies beneath. One critic commented on how 'her painted torsos assume an elemental air reminiscent of the stark hills and valleys above her home.' [18]

Working in the landscape offers the painter a tremendous freedom, but it also imposes strict, one could say impossible, challenges, best expressed by Cézanne, in September 1906, just a month before his death: 'Will I arrive at the goal, so intensely sought and so long pursued? I am working from nature, and it seems to me I am making slow progress.'

The interaction between our children and their friends gave Ghislaine a wealth of new and welcome subject matter. Cordelia was a very different child from Max, dark-haired and possessed of a fierce energy, even then brimming over with an irrepressible sense of the dramatic. Max, on the other hand, was blond-haired, and a dreamer, who spent much of his time living in his imaginary worlds. Separately and together they feature in so many of Ghislaine's paintings and drawings – and mine too – and these works are treasured memories of happy times.

With two small children, studio time became even more precious and what potentially might

Self-Portrait with Cordelia
1997
Acrylic on flax
127 x 101.6 cm
Collection of the Artist

relationship such as ours is a crucial enrichment of my practice. But there are days when I keep the studio door firmly shut – occasions, sometimes prolonged, when solitude and complete concentration are essential.

A number of her works from this time feature Ghislaine feeding or holding the children; these are often developed from very summary sketches, her own memories or snapshots taken by myself. A drawing now in the collection of the Whitworth Art Gallery is one such. Drawn on a roll of heavy–duty lining paper, it shows Ghislaine as she feeds Cordelia, looking down and drawing what she sees. It is a record of a touching and intimate moment of an artist at work. Ghislaine has torn the paper from the roll as she finished the drawing, letting it fall onto the studio floor, only to have our dog Tess come running in from the garden, straight across the paper, leaving her muddy paw prints as evidence of her intervention. A wonderful memory of a wonderful dog.

There are works of a more intimate nature too, for as Picasso once remarked, 'art is never chaste.'[19] Surely every artist has works that respond to their own private lives in one way or another. In Ghislaine's oeuvre there are a number of works ranging from Valentine cards to self-portraits, memory drawings and

have been a disadvantage only served to bring more focus into Ghislaine's working practice. It is a method of working that characterises her art to this day, fast, improvisational painting supported by time spent thinking and producing sheet after sheet of preparatory drawings – drawings of all kinds, speedy notations, quick jottings and more considered studies, all of which serve to prepare the ground for the moment when painting can begin in earnest.

It's an odd thing that working under pressure, of whatever kind, minimises a tendency to overwork. Broken patterns of working mean that paintings have time to rest and to be seen again later with fresh eyes. Sometimes it is them and not me that seem to decide whether they are finished or whether they demand that further work is necessary. Michael's has always been the critical voice that I respected most, but his frankness, though needed and welcomed, would have to be dealt with and any advice taken into account, whether accepted or rejected. I think that any artist needs to work with a certain amount of creative tension and everyone needs a sounding board; and the daily give and take of opinion and ideas that is inescapable in a

Richard Thomson
The Degasists
(left panel)
1987
Oil on canvas
142.2 x 116.8 cm
Courtesy of Gateway Gallery

Richard Kendall
The Degasists
(right panel)
1987
Oil on canvas
142.2 x 116.8 cm
Courtesy of Gateway Gallery

paintings that celebrate love and togetherness and also of course those moments that remind her of her own mortality and sensuality. Sometimes these are veiled as mythological subjects or homages to Persian miniatures, Japanese *Shunga*, pastiches of Picasso or sometimes scenes caught *sur le vif*.

In moving to Glossop, Ghislaine had set herself at a distance from those centres of influence that have shaped many successful careers, but for her, relative seclusion was necessary in order to keep and harness her individual voice. Her drawings and paintings are characterised by a drive to draw and paint as directly as possible without overt stylistic borrowings, to find a language or means appropriate to her needs – to allow her work to form itself.

As Max and Cordelia respected Ghislaine's work, so we respected and encouraged theirs. We valued Max's writing that grew out of his imaginary games and Cordelia's already evident love for drama and making art. Ghislaine painted and drew them in every aspect of their lives: asleep, learning to walk, at table, brushing their teeth, or playing in the garden with

their friends. Cordelia remembers: "It seemed entirely normal for us to be painted and drawn just doing normal things – eating a yoghurt, brushing our teeth – and have these captured in a quick drawing and then watching them turning into paintings. It is extraordinary to have my life mapped like that. It's very special to be able to look back on these paintings – so much better than photographs!"

Our friends must have known that every move they made and every walk we shared, every barbecue or outing, could end up incorporated into one of Ghislaine's paintings, however removed from the immediate source of inspiration that painting might be. Our friend Jem Waygood lost in reverie before an open fire or swimming with his children, Jack and Jessie – all became subjects for paintings.

The Books
At this time I was writing what was to become a steady stream of art books, mostly on various aspects of nineteenth-century art; a subject of obvious interest to Ghislaine who learnt much from the research and discussions that were an inevitable part of the writing process.

These began when, in 1988, I collaborated with Belinda Thomson to write a book on Impressionism. It was a delight to work with her and this opportunity opened the door for a number of other commissions. It is a privilege and deep joy to be able to publish on those artists whom one loves so much. Other books followed, one of the most significant of these publications was *The Impressionists by Themselves*. This book in particular affected us greatly, requiring as it did, a huge amount of research on their letters and memoirs and so there was much discussion in our household about those painters, their lives, ideas and works. Ghislaine found nourishment and inspiration from the information and anecdotes that came to light and not least what these very individualistic painters said or wrote about painting. We both became ever more aware of the complex nature of artistic creation and the pleasures that art can bring. The books were paralleled and informed by our travels to France and elsewhere. Art history was not, for us, an arid subject removed from practice, but embedded within it and central to our lives.

Michael Writing
1996
Oil on canvas
45.7 x 61 cm
Collection of the Artist

The Private Degas Exhibition

We shared with our friends a passionate regard for nineteenth-century French painting, above all for the art of Edgar Degas. Some key events of that time were Richard Thomson's exhibition at the Whitworth Art Gallery in 1987 entitled 'The Private Degas' and Richard Kendall's exhibition at the newly opened Liverpool Tate, 'Degas and Images of Women' (a title that parallels Ghislaine's 1983 exhibition at the Royal Exchange Theatre). These two breathtaking shows affirmed something Ghislaine had always felt: a kinship with Degas's commitment to the contingencies of the contemporary, whilst at the same time respecting and learning from other painters. Degas said, 'No art is less spontaneous than mine. What I do is the result of reflection and the study of the great masters; of inspiration, spontaneity, temperament ... I know nothing.'[20] An insight as concise as it is inspirational and one that has supported her practice to this day. Ghislaine enjoyed the discussions that were a consequence of my professional activities and we co-wrote an essay on Degas's

pastels for *The Artist* Magazine and Ghislaine authored articles about her own work for the same publication. Richard Kendall was fast becoming one of the world's leading authorities on Degas. We have fond memories of the moment when he emerged triumphant from the etching studio in the cellar of our house, having discovered after much effort the means by which Degas had achieved the mysterious effects of his magnificent landscape monotypes.

There was an engagement with television films such as Degas: *An Old Man Mad About Art* and most memorably, working once again with Richard Kendall and the film director Mischa Scorer, a film on *Degas and the Dance*, that was inspired by Richard and his partner Jill de Vonyar's revelatory exhibition of the same name that was showed in both Philadelphia and Detroit.[21] For the film, Ghislaine made a number of recreations of Degas oils and pastels whilst I worked with sculptors and printmaking students and friends to produce a number of 'Degas' etchings and monotypes as well as a veritable forest of wax sculptures.

'It's through Howard's moving embodiment of empathy with her subjects that she really makes her individual mark. And several images here... are so intimately tender in approach, they could hardly have been painted by any male, at any time, anywhere.'

Robert Clark, The Guardian, 29 March 1993

The Lowry Connection

All this concern with Impressionism enriched my thinking about L. S. Lowry and I became more and more convinced that his significance went well beyond that suggested by his popular image. I was already aware of him, of course, but mostly as part of Ghislaine's world as she had grown up with his work. However, it was not in Manchester or Salford, but in Newcastle that our first serious encounter with the phenomenon that was Lowry took place. Midway between the university and the polytechnic (now the University of Northumbria) was situated the Stone Gallery, a place of great fascination for us, for almost every day as students we would walk past it to meet each other for lunch and occasionally enter its shadowy interior. On the walls, amongst drawings by Henry Moore and other twentieth-century modernists we could see the lugubrious works by Rossetti, so beloved by Lowry. It was only many years later, talking with Tilly Marshall, the gallery's owner, about Lowry that she told me that as an old man, he would sit hidden by a curtain looking out at the 'pieces of totty' (his words), walking by. Given

Ghislaine's physical resemblance to Lowry's preferred type, he would probably have noticed her and commented upon her appearance.[22] But of this we knew nothing and it would be some time before Ghislaine would be able to make her own response to his work.

However, a number of artists she admired then and who have since become so well known, such as Lucian Freud, Frank Auerbach and Paula Rego, have all at some stage of their careers made evident their respect for Lowry as a 'painter's painter'.[23] This understanding was echoed by a number of brilliant writers as various as Sir Kenneth Clark, John Berger and others. Such figures recognised his qualities and the nature of his achievement, even if they understood that achievement in very different ways. In the years after his death in 1976, there was little agreement as to his status as an artist. Little did I know then that I would be the one to be given the task of reassessment.

For Ghislaine, Lowry's paintings were closely associated with childhood memories of visiting

Midwife Waiting to Receive the New Child
1993
Oil on flax
122 x 61 cm
Collection of the Artist

Salford Art Gallery. Her father often suggested that Lowry was the artist she should emulate, advice she had never really taken to heart, but now, as we visited Salford Art Gallery on a regular basis, so our appreciation of him grew ever deeper.

All this was viewed by my art historian colleagues with some dismay – even as something deliberately perverse – for the artist's name was never heard of within either of the two great educational institutions of Manchester: the Polytechnic (now Manchester School of Art) where Lowry had studied life drawing for so many years and Manchester University. This was troubling to me for Lowry's works seemed particularly relevant during this period, one of deep social and political unrest and especially during the years of 1984–5, when the miners' struggle was so much in the news. Though Lowry would have had little sympathy for their cause.

Shire Hill Hospital

For a number of years Ghislaine had been a regular visitor to Glossop's Shire Hill Hospital drawing the elderly people in the day care centre. The birth of Max and Cordelia had triggered a deep emotional realisation in her that as we are born, so we grow old and die. She felt it almost a duty to make something of this fascination with extreme youth and extreme old age – to give it visual form. To make sense, if she could, of what she and our children

would one day become. Once she began work at the hospital she found innumerable parallels between what she herself had experienced in the maternity unit and the Special Care Unit at Saint Mary's and what she met with at the hospital in Glossop. The determination of a

Newly Born Baby
1993
Oil on board
51 x 43 cm
Manchester Art Gallery

Hugo Ball
1994
Oil on panel
20.3 x 15.2 cm
Manchester Metropolitan University

stroke victim learning to walk again, sheltered by the protecting gesture of a nurse for example, led to a number of major paintings, the care that one person can show. 'The kindness of strangers' – a theme that concerns Ghislaine to this day. Not only did this experience answer some of her own private concerns, but she also saw the good it did for those with whom she worked, both those attending the day centre and the staff who cared for them.

The Shared Experience Exhibition

It was never enough for Ghislaine just to paint her own domestic life, or to make studies from painters, past and present, that she admired. Her ambition was steady, but difficult to achieve. Like the Impressionists, like Lowry, indeed, she wished to paint works that were part of the larger social realities of the day. Like them, she felt a need to respond to Baudelaire's still relevant question: 'Where is the painter of modern life?'[24] In fact, as Manet, Degas and countless others have realised, it is all around us – the trick is to find the right way of approaching it and for many it is by beginning from one's immediate surroundings and working outwards.

My radar is always attuned to seek out any artists from whom I can learn or with whom I can claim, privately, a kind of fellowship. I had

always been an admirer of Kitaj's drawings, his spare and precise draughtsmanship and the frankness of his imagery. And over the years, I became increasingly aware of women painters Ana Maria Pacheco, Jenny Saville and Eileen Cooper, for example, and later, Marline Dumas – all artists who were treating similar subjects and ideas as those that attracted me, but with very different results. And I have been often taken aback at unexpected connections that I find in works that are often very removed from my own.

Ghislaine found herself revisiting the preoccupations of her earliest years, drawing old people and through her experience as a mother considering the idea of painting the very beginnings of life as a definite plan. In 1992, as a result of such thoughts, she approached Manchester Art Gallery with the idea of an exhibition relating to these two areas of human experience. After some time she heard that they her proposal had been accepted, but they wanted her to limit her activities to charting and interpreting hospital birth.

For a period of four months, Ghislaine visited Saint Mary's Maternity Unit in Manchester to research and develop a large body of work which formed the basis of an exhibition at Manchester Art Gallery entitled, 'A Shared Experience'. Here was modern life, but an aspect of modern life that had rarely, if ever, been pictured. It also gave opportunity, as we realised later, to engage with some of the great formal structures of past art and discover

resonances and parallels with the great Biblical narratives that had inspired such painters as Giotto, Masaccio and Rembrandt.[25]

It was a challenge to establish a meaningful rapport with the staff and mothers-to-be in order to do justice to her brief, to work with them from the antenatal clinic through to the delivery room and after. These works recall not only the immediacy, urgency and drama of all the events connected with hospital birth, but as ever with Ghislaine's work, the evocative gestures of nurses, mothers-to-be and the doctors, recall and draw power from, the language of earlier art.

She told Jane Fickling in an article for the *The Daily Telegraph*:

I'm not a distant observer. I think the close-up gives a sense of immediacy. For instance, the midwife's hands, or the surgeon's back and other parts of the body are just as expressive as the face.[26]

The opening of the exhibition was a quite wonderful occasion, for not only was there the usual assembly of art lovers, Friends of the Gallery etc., but also present were the mothers and their babies whom Ghislaine had worked with, together with the midwives, doctors and other members of staff from the hospital. The innovative nature of the exhibition drew the attention of the Wellcome Foundation and in 1994 the whole sequence of works were shown at their London Gallery complex on Euston Road.

Art critic Robert Clark wrote in *The Guardian*: 'Here are paintings entitled

Inserting the Catheter, Before the Caesarean and Breech Birth. If it weren't for the subject matter Howard might fit neatly within the British serious painterly tradition of Bomberg, Auerbach and Kossoff.... So it's through Howard's moving embodiment of empathy with her subjects that she really makes her individual mark. And several images here – for instance one painting entitled Second Day showing a baby's top heavy sleeping head, already weary with the weight of life, cradled in the mother's giant hands – are so intimately tender in approach, they could hardly have been painted by any male, at any time, anywhere.'[27]

The whole experience of working for the exhibition and the overwhelmingly positive responses it received, prompted Ghislaine to consider another long-held ambition. As so often happens in her career it is fascinating how one specific project can spill over to suggest another, apparently unconnected, set of ideas. Certain moments and images witnessed at the maternity unit brought back remembered scenes from the *Stations of the Cross* that Ghislaine had known since childhood and she began to consider the idea of making her own response to that time-honoured subject.

Risley Prison Residency and the Year of Drama

As a direct result of the Manchester exhibition, Ghislaine was approached by the education office of Risley Prison to work towards co-ordinating an exhibition of her own work and that of a group of male inmates. Ghislaine organised workshops to inspire the men to create work as she developed her own paintings and drawings in response to her time there. The resulting exhibition at Warrington Art Gallery was entitled 'Inside Out'.

I decided to use the idea of the separateness of prison life as the basis of the workshops. I was determined to intervene as little as possible, to facilitate an exploration of their own sense of identity. We began with simple drawing exercises. Using their own hands and faces the group began to explore the idea of portraiture; how images could convey not only a likeness but also something of their private and public selves.

In 1994 Manchester was chosen as the European City of Drama, for which I produced a dramatic re-presentation at the university of material first performed in Zürich at the Cabaret Voltaire in 1916 by the Dadaists, and Ghislaine recognised an opportunity too good to be missed. She not only charted the development of the project, but also worked with the Royal Exchange Theatre, the Contact Theatre and other venues to produce an exhibition at the British Council the following year entitled, '*Caught in the Act*'. But it was the recreation of the Cabaret Voltaire that most excited her. Together with my then research assistant, Debbie Lewer, and with the help of colleagues from across the university, as well as students from Stockport College of Art, we rebuilt to the original floor plan the space in which the Dadaists gave their nightly performances. Ghislaine drew and painted the actors in rehearsal as they took on the roles of Hugo Ball, Emmy Hennings, Tristan Tzara, Hans Arp and Richard Heulsenbeck. She was amazed, not only at the energy and inventiveness of the actors, but also stunned by the nature of the material itself. Dada is frequently misunderstood – but that is the nature of the beast. Hans Arp explained: 'While guns rumbled in the distance, we sang, painted, made collages and wrote poems with all our might. We were seeking an art based on fundamentals, to cure the madness of the age, and find a new order of things that would restore the balance between heaven and hell.'[28]

We have both taken this to heart.

These two events proved to be important in the development of Ghislaine's art in a number of ways, for the world of the hospital, the prison and the theatre have much in common. Following a close involvement with director Annie Castledine and the actor Josette Bushelmingo on a production of *The Threepenny Opera* in Manchester, Ghislaine was invited to follow the progress of the National Theatre's 1995 production of Euripedes' *Women of Troy*. Inspired by Don McCullin's war photography, the resulting production was visceral in the extreme. Working with actors in rehearsal, watching them find the right physical language to express intense emotional states was a very powerful experience for Ghislaine. She also found inspirational the ways in which the actors

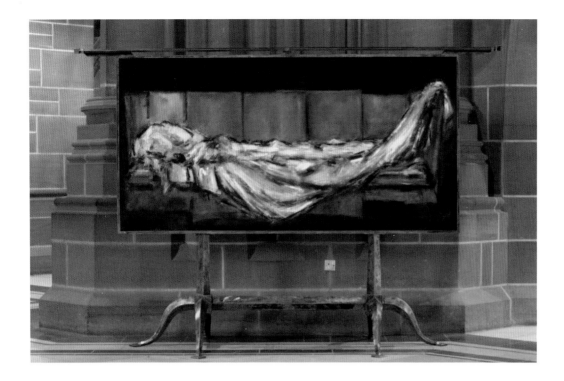

The Empty Tomb
Liverpool Cathedral
(Steel reliquary designed and
made by Brian Fell)
2008

sustained periods of prolonged concentration and physical activity, only to collapse into each other's arms at the end of a particularly gruelling scene or action.

Here was a world in which the real and the artificial collided and intertwined. The energy of the rehearsal room with its moment of release and control, the juxtaposition of spontaneous actions and strictly controlled ones was a continual source of inspiration for me.

Every painting is built upon the last, each a risk-taking, each only part of a cumulative process. As she works, Ghislaine is always ready to recognise the resonances that occur between the sometimes very disparate paintings she might be producing at any one time. By preference she chooses to have her work all about her whilst she paints. As she was working on the painting of a young man in the segregation unit in Risley Prison for example, she was reminded of a painting she had made of Max asleep, safe within the security of the family home. The image of the sleeping figure is

a recurrent theme in Ghislaine's work as is the figure who turns away, averting their gaze from that of the viewer; a common subject in the history of art as it creates an immediate sense of vulnerability, ambiguity and mystery.

Stations of the Cross / The Captive Figure

The back room of our house, which had been the old tripe works, was in a state of imminent collapse and had to be demolished and rebuilt in 1987. We had dreams of a tiny cloistered garden, but through the help of a local builder we were able to save it as a building and once complete, it became Ghislaine's main studio space. She retains a vivid memory of bringing Cordelia home for the first time and having to negotiate a treacherous terrain of stone and timber that lay strewn about the courtyard. The only consolation was knowing that in the fullness of time this debris would be transformed into a place of work.

Once it was completed, the new studio

became the venue for a communal life drawing session that ran on a weekly basis. We found a number of excellent models including one of my colleagues, an art historian, life model and great friend, Chris Ackroyd. His dedication to and participation in the classes led Ghislaine to ask him to collaborate on a series of drawings relating to the *Stations of the Cross*. So for a number of years Chris would come out to the studio and enact the progress of Christ from his trial to his entombment, even agreeing to be crucified – if only for a few seconds.

There is nothing like drawing the life model to make one sensitive to the complexities of the gaze. Ghislaine imagined herself in the position of someone within the crowd witnessing the tragic events unfold before her. Drawing after drawing followed over the next few years with Chris acting out each of the 14 *Stations* in turn. Ghislaine made the decision not to show Christ's face as it was important to her that these works should not be so much religious as humanitarian in spirit. The particular nature of the sequence's title makes this evident, for this was everyman, a victim of a corrupt judicial procedure, forced to undergo a humiliating and terrifying series of events that would lead to his eventual murder. A high point in our lives came when Dan Jones of Amnesty International visited Ghislaine's studio to see the work in progress and asked if Amnesty could use the images as part of their activities.

Doctor John Elford, Rector of Liverpool Hope University, saw the drawings and commissioned Ghislaine to produce a series of large paintings developed from them.

I am happiest working on a large scale. Painting is a very physical activity for me – my whole arm goes into it. I like to feel the energy work its way through my body. It is as if, at each point of contact with the canvas, an imaginary circuit is completed that, I hope, sparks into life when seen by the viewer.

Ghislaine decided to produce the works as monochrome canvases, mixing her paint with sand to give an added texture to the paintings' surface. The drawing is broadly handled, using great arcing movements to capture the drama of the narrative and to allow its choreographic elements to come to the fore, so that the abstract and the figurative qualities of each painting operate together to create a unified assault upon the viewer's sensibilities.

In 2000 the completed works were shown at Liverpool Cathedral and at the other end of Hope Street, at the Metropolitan Cathedral, a group of corresponding witness figure were shown. The *Stations* have continued to tour the cathedrals of the UK ever since. At each venue they have elicited very moving responses from Christians and non-Christians alike. Sister Wendy Beckett wrote that 'Ghislaine Howard's work has a passionate roughness that seems sublimely right for the pain and confusion of the Passion. The *Stations* cry out to the viewer/ prayer the meaning of human cruelty and our rejection of God's gentleness and love.'[29]

Others centred upon the universal relevance of the humanitarian aspect of the subject matter. Helen Bamber, the founder of the charity The Medical Foundation for the Care of Victims of Torture, said the following at the opening event of an exhibition of the *Stations* at Canterbury Cathedral, 'Ghislaine Howard's images are compelling, powerful, and emphatic. They are unusual in that they communicate man's inhumanity to man to the art lover and lay person alike. These are very important paintings that transcend the limitations of the gallery space to speak to us all.'

The work has been recognised by political refugees, brought solace to the bereaved and elicited positive responses from people of all ages and all walks of life. Such response gives credence to Francis Bacon's point about the resonance of this subject: 'One knows how very potent some of the images of Christianity have been and how deeply they play on one's sensibility. So one can never say that one has got completely away from it.'[30]

Saint Anthony Meets Saint Paul
(detail from the Saint Anthony sequence)
2002

The Studio at Oak Street
(with works in progress for the Saint Anthony sequence)
2002

Many people responded to the paintings as they would to any other works of art, commenting on their appreciation of their aesthetic qualities alone, ignoring the very particular nature of the subject matter. Whatever form they may take, the comments in the visitors' books have been overwhelmingly favourable and surprisingly varied. One or two, however, it must be said, echo the thoughts of Ghislaine's art teacher at Adelphi House!

In 2004 in recognition of the Queen's visit to Gloucester Cathedral for the Royal Maundy Thursday service, a study from the series was presented to Her Majesty and is now in the Royal Collection. The choice of subject was left open to Ghislaine and a study for the *Lamentation of the Women of Jerusalem* was graciously accepted during an informal reception in the Deanery and Ghislaine received a special fee – the traditional amount of seven pence in tiny silver coins.

The Empty Tomb

In 2008 Liverpool was named as European Capital of Culture and early in 2007 it was decided by the Cathedral that the *Stations* should be shown again to celebrate this event, but that they should be completed by the addition of a final painting. The Resurrection was mooted as a possible subject, but Ghislaine suggested instead the subject of the Empty Tomb as an image that would speak more eloquently to a wider audience – for this resting place could be that of the Risen Christ, or a rough sleeper, or even one of the 'disappeared'. We walked the precincts of both cathedrals on Easter Monday just before dawn, and in one of the imposing doorways of the Catholic Metropolitan Cathedral, Ghislaine saw a heap of rags and cardboard. As we stopped in the half-light, she noticed a slight movement and realised that this was someone's bed and that they were still asleep. The contrast between spiritual and material realities could not have been more sharply drawn to our attention and this encounter gave fire to Ghislaine's determination to ensure that the painting, whatever form it would take, would preserve something of that moment.

The Saint Anthony Commission

This major sequence of works was commissioned in 2001 for a stately home in North Yorkshire. The subject requested was the Life of Saint Anthony to be comprised of six large arched panels, specially constructed to fit a beautiful eighteenth-century orangery. Family and friends found themselves prevailed upon to participate in studies for the paintings – as well as a camel from Chester Zoo. One of the most challenging episodes to paint was the meeting of the young Saint Anthony with the elderly Saint Paul, the subject of a famous painting by Velàsquez. Ghislaine's painting features Robin Thornber and Max, not to mention a centaur and a blackbird delivering a fresh loaf of bread to the aged saint.

Ghislaine has fond memories of working with Robin, who posed for Saint Paul. He was a gentle, generous man with a real sense of community spirit. He wore his white hair long and looked every inch a Biblical patriarch, and as the ex-drama critic of *The Guardian* newspaper, the irony of this was not lost on us, but these looks made him the obvious choice for the role. Robin turned up on the first day with his head shaved, his magnificent locks sacrificed for charity the evening before. Bald and wearing sandals, shorts and a flowery Hawaiian shirt, he looked as unbiblical as one could imagine. Ghislaine had a problem, but, scouring the studio cupboards, she unearthed an old Driza-Bone coat and in a moment the New Testament saint stood before her and work got underway.

'Ghislaine Howard's images are compelling, powerful, and emphatic. These are very important paintings that transcend the limitations of the gallery space to speak to us all.'

Helen Bamber, founder of the charity The Medical Foundation for the Care of Victims of Torture.

From the 365 Series
Oil on board
15.25 x 20.3 cm
Collection of the Artist

Self-Portrait with Max
1985
Oil on Canvas
121.9 x 91.4 cm
Collection of the Artist

The Visitation Altarpiece

Ever since her first encounter as a student with Delacroix's *Jacob Wrestling with the Angel*, Ghislaine had harboured an unspoken ambition to paint on a monumental scale for a public building. Fulfilment of such a dream seemed highly unlikely, if not impossible, but in 2003, it came to pass when Liverpool Hope University offered her a commission for a large painting for Saint Katherine's Chapel (now renamed Trinity Chapel) situated at the heart of the Hope Park campus. When built in 1930 it was planned that one day the end wall of the chapel (over 30 feet in height) would be 'enriched in colour and texture by a painting to be situated in the large arched space behind the altar'.[31] Ghislaine suggested that the Visitation would be apposite. After much preparatory work, in May 2003 Ghislaine began to draw directly upon the pitted surface of the wall and the painting, 25 feet in height, was completed six weeks later in July in time for that year's student graduation ceremony. A few days before that event, Ghislaine's family gathered in the chapel to see the completed work. Her brother Mike played the piano and glasses were raised in celebration. Her father, though lost in his own world of dementia, offered her for the first time in her life, a response of complete approbation. His eyes brimming with tears, he said, 'It's wonderful, I wouldn't change a thing.' This moment was made even more poignant when he continued a moment later, 'I'll just go upstairs and tell my mother.'

The painting brings together many of the concerns that recur throughout Ghislaine's work. It depicts the very moment of the meeting of Mary and her elder relative,

Elizabeth, both are pregnant, Mary with Jesus and Elizabeth with John the Baptist. It is at once an intensely spiritual and human moment. Although monumental in scale, this is an intimate encounter. The intimacy of their meeting is expressed through a hierarchical gesture. As the two women embrace, Elizabeth rests her hand on Mary's side to feel the movement of her child.

Family Life

We lived in an atmosphere in which creativity and the full play of the imagination was central to our everyday lives. I wrote and illustrated stories with Max, whilst Cordelia was never happier than when she was making paintings, peg dolls or jewellery out of nutshells and bits of worn glass. Max lived a large part of his early childhood in a variety of extraordinary imaginary worlds and was always more interested in writing, inventing and cataloguing demons and monsters and their domains. Cordelia, like ourselves, has always loved to paint and draw, often in direct competition with myself. Always resourceful; if no empty canvases were to hand, she would disappear down into the cellar picture store, only to appear a little later with a painting in her hand and innocently inquire, 'You don't want this one, do you?' And then to add insult to injury, she would have the effrontery to shut us out of the kitchen, her workplace of choice, whilst she painted over it.

As younger children, Max and Cordelia thought nothing of growing up in a family home where the kitchen window gave access to the studio space where any number of Ghislaine's works in progress could be seen.

However, given the nature of some of the paintings, if one of their friends was coming to tea perhaps, there might be a request to 'turn that one round'.

Max and Cordelia's engagement with Ghislaine's art changed over the years. As they grew older so they took a more active role in a number of major works. Max is immediately recognisable in the Saint Anthony sequence, but in *Stations of the Cross*, only his feet are visible, emerging from swathes of cloth in the final canvas of the series, Christ Entombed. Likewise, Cordelia has appeared in many guises, including that of Saint Anthony's young sister and as Mary in the Visitation altarpiece, wearing the very clothes that her mother had worn in her Pregnant *Self-Portrait, July 1984*. Ghislaine herself posed for the figure of Elizabeth.

Travels

Like theatre directors, artists have to know how to make bodies and gestures eloquent. Working with people that she has known for a long time has allowed Ghislaine to build up a visual repertoire of the ways in which bodies express emotions through their gestures and physical attitudes. Often, the turn of the head or the fall of a shoulder can suggest far more than a fleeting facial expression. It is for her an everyday practice to be looking out for those unguarded moments, when the stances that people fall into somehow 'speak' to her. These moments, that are such a feature of Degas's working practice, give an eloquence to the human body that can only be caught in the midst of life itself. When such a moment is registered, the task then is to catch it as

These works fell quite naturally into the thematic rhythms of Ghislaine's work: birth, life and the inevitability of death. Sadly, Martin died in 2004. Ghislaine produced a touching portrait of three generations standing together in silent grief: her mother, herself and our daughter Cordelia.

quickly and discreetly as possible, in a quick sketch or snapshot perhaps, to preserve as an aide-memoire for future use. Such moments are often encountered in railway stations, at bus stops or in a café or pub – anywhere in fact, where people gather, meet and bid their farewells. One of the best times for doing this is on holiday. We remember our family camping trips to France, at first under canvas, but most memorably in our Conway Tardis, a strange vehicle that was in essence a fold-up caravan with cantilevered sleeping areas. Its large plastic windows transformed everything into an Impressionist painting. Our stays at Normandy and Brittany were caught informally in sketchbooks and small oils that Ghislaine would later work up into more finished compositions.

Although we visited and painted the sights where Monet and Braque worked in Pourville, Varengeville and elsewhere, and followed the footsteps of Gauguin in and around Pont-Aven, we also travelled around Britain. In England, we enjoyed holidays in Mortehoe, the Lake District and North Wales, but Ireland was always in the background. For me, it held

memories of my early childhood in the North and for Ghislaine, there was their cottage on the outskirts of Birr, right in the centre of the Republic. Across the river from their cottage was an early nineteenth-century whisky distillery, fallen into dereliction. On learning that the building was in danger of being demolished, Ghislaine's parents negotiated with 'Young' Hoare (who was then in his eighties) to buy it. This came about and the mill became their Irish home and over years, one of its remaining wings was transformed from a farm store into a basic but spectacular living space. A number of items came across from the old cottage including a terracotta mask that would become the starting point for Ghislaine's first Irish exhibition in 2010. These trips to Ireland were supplemented by time spent with friends in London and in New York, where we would visit my childhood friend, Alastair Noble and his wife, Kathy Bruce, both artists based in Manhattan but with a small house upstate. This friendship has lead to many creative collaborations, most memorably at the Experimental Print Institute at Lafayette College, Pennsylvania.

The Continuing Impact of Lowry

Life continually takes us by surprise, and no more so than when my interest in the work of L. S. Lowry began to bear fruit. A friend from my student days in Newcastle, Virginia Tandy, then just at the beginning of her career as a curator, asked me to write an essay for an exhibition of Lowry's work in Stalybridge Art Gallery, a few miles from the artist's last home in Mottram. This in turn led to my becoming more engaged with his work, professionally, giving lectures about him in London and elsewhere, and in 1998 I was commissioned to write the first major monograph on the artist. I worked with the newly founded Lowry Centre at Salford Quays, then merely a massive hole in the ground surrounded by derelict land at the end of the Manchester Ship Canal. It was the very landscape that had so fascinated Ghislaine back in the 1980s that was now being redeveloped as a major cultural centre.

Working with the Lowry material taught us both a great deal; it not only shaped our professional lives, but affected our personal

Flowers for my Father
(study)
2004
Oil on board
61 x 61 cm
Collect Art

lives too. For me, there was the shock of discovering the nature and significance of Lowry's erotic work. For Ghislaine, there was the realisation of how certain aspects of his work had filtered through into her concerns, particularly the walking figures. My research made me especially sensitive about issues relating to the relationship between an artist's public and private life, their ideas and concerns, and how that relates to understanding and interpreting artwork. For example, it made us consider the idea of 'authorship' – that is, the artist's relationship to their work. For though Ghislaine's paintings are painted by her and stem from her hand and relate in some way

to her life, it has to be borne in mind that the maker of a painting is normally absent from the work when it is viewed and so, to some degree, it stands alone, 'outside' her biography.

Paintings have their own life and are interpreted differently according to the circumstances in which they are seen. A good example of this are the works that Ghislaine painted in response to a three-month Arts Council funded residency at Glossop Women's Refuge in 2000.[32] The resulting paintings and drawings, a woman making tea, putting her child to bed, or just watching television, may seem very ordinary to an outsider. But once

the context is realised, these happenings that seem so mundane become charged with extra significance.

It was deeply moving for me to realise that these ordinary everyday activities that I took for granted were something that these women had been denied – but here, in a place of support and safety, they could be once more be enjoyed as a simple everyday occurrence.

Looking at such images reminds us that we are storytelling creatures. We share stories and interpret them according to our circumstances. Exploring paintings is one of the ways we learn about the world and test our assumptions against those suggested by others: so a painting is an open field for interpretative play – like going to a theatre or reading a novel. But what seems to come through most strongly for viewers of Ghislaine's work is a direct sense of emotional engagement, an empathy for the human condition; ideas that have shaped her belief that art, like music, can transcend the sometimes limited power of words.

However, paintings are not sermons or homilies; they are objects that work through the visual, their impact, immediate and lasting, is through the beauty and potency of colour, line, shape and form working together. They are vessels of compressed energy, the trace of the artist's hand caught in the paint revealing the individuality and distinctiveness of the artist's voice. So the single image may contain a concealed strength and unleash emotional responses which can be unexpected and unforeseen by the artist. For one person, an image of a child sleeping may be an occasion for simple delight but for another, it might release emotions or memories too complex to articulate fully. Ghislaine was told of a client who bought a portrait of Cordelia asleep. On taking it home, she said that she had felt a sudden sense of release that at last, her daughter, who had died some years before, had 'come home', and as a result felt a certain peace fall upon her grief. Such moments cannot be adequately expressed in words. Equally, a

simple embrace – is it a meeting or departure? An image of joy, pleasure, support or sorrow, anguish or just plain exhaustion? It depends on who is looking at it and with what purpose.

I want to make my art sing. A lovely phrase used by so many painters. To paint myself into the world as in different ways, quilt makers and the storytellers of old have done. Perhaps my work is a defence against the world or perhaps a way of recognising it in all its fullness. Who knows? Myself least of all.

Even Ghislaine admits that she does not have the knowledge necessary to explain away her own works – and that is how it should be, for art overflows biography as a child outgrows its parents and as water escapes a bubbling fountain.

The New Studio & Family Matters

In 2001, Ghislaine began to rent a studio on the ground floor of a dilapidated Victorian stable block in the back streets of Glossop. It had been constructed in the 1850s to house the dray horses that once delivered goods from the Co-op to the people of the town. Now it stood in need of urgent repair, but it fulfilled Ghislaine's immediate needs for a larger working space. The move coincided with her parents expressing their desire to move out to Glossop. Her mother was suffering from Parkinson's Disease and the seriousness of Martin's protracted illness was becoming evermore apparent. However, these sad

occurrences had an unexpected outcome for Ghislaine. She found that she was able to draw and paint her parents in a way that had not been previously possible. Innumerable sketches and some key paintings record something of their deep love for each other and shared vulnerability to the changing realities of their lives. These works, though intensely personal, reach beyond the particular circumstances of their making to express what are surely universal feelings. Though unlooked for, these works fell quite naturally into the thematic rhythms of Ghislaine's work: birth, life and the inevitability of death. The move to Glossop was decided upon and accordingly the stables were purchased and, over the next year or so, were restored and the upper floor converted into a spacious apartment. Sadly, Martin died in June 2004, and from a number of snapshots taken at his funeral in Birr, Ghislaine produced a touching portrait of three generations standing together in silent grief: her mother, herself and our daughter Cordelia.

Now that Maureen was alone, the family rallied round to ensure that her life would be as comfortable and secure as possible. Though physically frail, she had a will of iron and made light of her illness. She decided not to move to Glossop, but instead she found a smaller

house close to the old family home, finding
new friends and rediscovering old ones. As the
new apartment was no longer needed, it was
agreed that we should convert it into a gallery
space. Ghislaine relished taking work out of
the studio and into the clean open areas of
what was now a light-filled gallery. She could
also be present as people saw and responded to
her paintings, and enjoy a direct relationship
with viewers that painters rarely experience. I
exhibited my paintings as did Cordelia and a
small group of fellow artists, including Eileen
Cooper, who had been born and raised in
Glossop, and Ian Mood who has become a
great friend and painting companion. We sold
work and organised weekend courses, but there
was a measure of relief when the building was
eventually sold and we were able to concentrate
our energies on our own home, restructuring
it to suit our changed circumstances now
that both Max and Cordelia were living
independent lives in Manchester and London.

The 365 Series

Ghislaine has never been a programmatic
painter, but one who is stirred by basic human
emotions and then follows their drift. She

doesn't operate to a preconceived plan, but once an idea for a project or a particular painting strikes her, she takes it to heart and follows it through to completion.

On 6 July 2005, Ghislaine travelled down to London for a meeting at St Paul's Cathedral the following day. She was staying with an old friend in London, and on the morning of 7 July she visited the Rebecca Horne exhibition at the Hayward Gallery, completely unaware of the terrible events that were unfolding just a mile or so away. However, we at home knew that she could well have been passing through the very streets where the atrocities unfolded.[33] Communication of any kind proved impossible and we were left in a state of confusion and anxiety. When we finally managed to make contact, Ghislaine told us of how on her return to her friend's house she had witnessed a trivial domestic dispute involving her friend's teenage son escalate into a violent altercation, to which

the police were called. The contrast between these two events was almost too much to bear.

On returning home, she attempted to make sense of that terrible day by painting it out of her system. To some extent she succeeded, but she found the paintings themselves unsatisfactory and they were destroyed. A year later, she saw the news photographs recalling the events of that day and she remembers:

Reading about the day in my daily newspaper I was struck by photographs in which the familiar streets of London had become the backdrop to horror. At that time I made a number of small paintings in response to these images and, almost without realising it, I had begun what would become a daily practice. Each day I choose one image (usually from The Guardian newspaper) that strikes a particular chord with me and make a small painting from it. Each panel is 6 x 8 inches. I try to paint them as simply and as

lovingly as I can. They have become an act of vigil – a way of giving time back to these images and the individuals represented in them. Feeling powerless in the face of world events, this is one thing I can do. When I started making the series I intended to continue each day for a year – now I see no reason to stop.[34]

And so her practice continues to this day. These were at first private paintings, a way of giving respect and time to images that have become disposable in our news-saturated culture. For Ghislaine, the works are also partly a meditation on the events pictured, a way of giving back some time to those figures or events represented. And not least, they operate as a means of preparing herself for the day's painting. The photographs she chooses to work from are not necessarily political, but simply the ones that strike her most vividly. Her manner of responding to each image is direct, even prosaic. It is the process that is

Gait Lab Study: Walking
(opposite top)
2010
Oil on panel
15.25 x 35.6 cm
Collect Art

Gait Lab Study (I)
(opposite bottom)
2010
Ink on paper
25.3 x 25.3 cm
Collect Art

important and not the final result. She often chooses a detail, not the main event itself, but a peripheral figure or action.

These small paintings accrued in her studio and a group of them were seen by Michael Simpson, then curator at the recently opened Imperial War Museum North in Salford, and he suggested that they should be shown there as a single entity. Interestingly, the building's architect, the American Daniel Libeskind, said that in thinking about the nature and purpose of the museum, he had sought to: 'create a building ... which emotionally moved the soul of the visitor toward a sometimes unexpected realization'[35] – which is exactly what Ghislaine has had as her ambition for so many years. The resulting exhibition of 365 of these panels took place in 2009 and was called quite simply the *365 Series*. Very occasionally something in one

of these images is developed into a larger work, but normally the practice stands alone as a separate entity.

Since then, they have continued to be exhibited in many different kinds of venue. When seen in such places as galleries, places of education, cathedrals, and public spaces of various kinds, questions are inevitably raised concerning how we deal with images of conflict, for many of the panels are responses to images of war or its aftermath.

At one exhibition, we learnt that a young boy, a refugee who had not spoken since his arrival in England, was prompted to do so, at length, by his encounter with them. Another memorable occasion was when 200 of the panels were exhibited in the Dutch Masters' room at Manchester Art Gallery, creating a dialogue

with the old masters and the celebrated *Last Supper* photographs of the contemporary artist Mat Collishaw.[36] Such interactions justify Picasso's belief that, 'there is no past or future in art. The art of the great painters who lived in other times is not an art of the past; perhaps it is more alive today than it ever was.'

The Exhibition At Birr: 'The Circus Animals' Desertion'

In 2010, Ghislaine was approached to hold an exhibition in Birr as part of their annual arts festival. Not far from our family home in Ireland, stands the beautiful tower that was Yeats's home – Thoor Ballylee. Its proximity gave his writing a special significance to us. Ghislaine took this opportunity to respond to this fact and she gathered together works that she had been making over the years inspired,

Welcome the Stranger
(study)
2015
Oil on canvas
101.6 x 91.4 cm
Collection of the Artist

however loosely, by Yeats's poetry and she also created a number of specific paintings and prints, relating to his late poem, 'The Circus Animals' Desertion'. Amongst these were *The Artist in Her Studio* and a series of images of blindfolded self-portraits. The poem has long been a favourite of ours and the poet's clear-eyed dissection of his own failed ambitions never fails to impress and inspire us.

Maureen

During this period, Ghislaine had spent a lot of time with her mother and recorded the last days she spent in the old house. She remembers particularly well a blazing hot July day, when Maureen made her farewells to the empty rooms, moving slowly and with great effort from cellar to attic. Her mother, determined but walking with difficulty and stopping now and then to pick up a piece of paper or to set something in place. Such movements became enormously poignant for Ghislaine as her mother, unaware, seemed to dance through the

mote-filled spaces. As she moved through the rooms, it was as if an old woman, physically challenged, had become once more a young girl.

These events inspired Ghislaine to produce a number of paintings of her mother moving through the house and as she worked on them, ideas connected to Yeats's poem converged and the idea came about for Ghislaine to move through our house in Glossop from cellar to attic, blindfolded, feeling her way. Why this suggested itself, she does not know, but somehow it felt an appropriate thing to do. Ghislaine repeated this action several times in different circumstances. In covering one's eyes, one protects oneself whilst at the same time acknowledging a certain vulnerability. The blindfold is also an image of great poetic power, for in not seeing outwardly, perhaps one looks inwards and puts faith in touch and hesitancy, and the familiar is made strange. These images, distilled as ever from countless sketches,

negotiate what can't be said directly, if at all. As Emily Dickinson wrote: 'because I could not say it – I fixed it in the verse – for you to read'.[37]

The Choreography of Walking

These experiences, combined with time spent in 2010–11 drawing at Salford University's Podiatry department, led to a sustained campaign to capture the magic and complexity of movement. A long admirer of Rodin's *Age of Bronze*, (1876) the idea of walking, and the body in movement was one that holds special significance for Ghislaine. Seeing Masaccio's *Expulsion* (c.1425) in Florence had been a singularly powerful moment in our younger lives. And so it was a moving experience to witness at Salford the determination of young children with cerebral palsy as they walked with difficulty back and forth between two fixed points, their every move recorded and interpreted by cameras and computers. Ghislaine did the same using the oldest of

technologies – pencil, paint and brush, moving with them whilst responding to their individual passage across the room as rapidly as she could. When the two points of reference were compared, one of the specialists commented as he looked at Ghislaine's 30–foot long drawing, 'Now that has caught the essence of walking.' An unintentional recognition of the power of a 30,000-year-old human practice. The resulting exhibition at the Salford University's Chapman Gallery brought together works from various stages of Ghislaine's career, all of which focused on different aspects of the 'Choreography of Walking'.

The Seven Acts Of Mercy

In early January 2012, to recharge our energies and draw a line under what had been a severe disappointment regarding the funding of a major commission, we decided to make a pilgrimage to Madrid. There, not only did we see the paintings we loved so much, not least the newly restored frescoes by Goya at the San Antonio Basilica, but also Velásquez's paintings in the Prado and the El Grecos at Toledo. As ever, these were stupendous in their impact, but it was coming across two small medieval panels depicting episodes from the Seven Acts of Mercy that triggered for Ghislaine an immediate and overwhelming emotional kick. Over coffee afterwards we realised that here was something special – a subject that related powerfully to everything she believed in and corresponded so closely to her daily 365 paintings. From this moment, the idea of producing seven major works dedicated to the subject took form. Ghislaine would continue the *365 Series*, but begin to actively seek out parallels in those images that recorded the presence, or more often, the absence, of the qualities of mercy or compassion. We are sure that observing and recording the care and compassion shown at Salford University's Podiatry department contributed to this decision.

There is always the question: why should the world be the way it is? And so, quietly, persistently, the *365 Series* suggested another avenue of activity. Paintings don't tell, but they can show and perhaps encourage others to act. Painting should and must reach out into the real world. Working with Shannon

Individual works may stand alone, but when set within Ghislaine's oeuvre, certain themes and recurring motifs become evident. Foremost amongst them, a respect for life and death in all its many aspects and the never-ending enigma of the identity of the self. All such visual and thematic connections create a powerful linkage between her early and late work.

Ledbetter and Blackburn College, Ghislaine was able to test whether this might be the case. Blackburn became a testing ground for something much more ambitious, and learning from the response of people in the city, young and old, from different social, religious or ethnic backgrounds, she realised that the idea worked. We grouped a number of paintings from Ghislaine's *365 Series* into sets of seven, each panel corresponding to one of the Acts of Mercy and then gave them to different communities to work with over a period of time. These panels were then exchanged with another group and conversations began. We have had encouraging results from Blackburn, South Africa and elsewhere which are shaping the future of this particular aspect of Ghislaine's work.

A Time Of Change
An artist's life is a precarious one, and Ghislaine in particular, feels a continuing need to prove herself against her own exacting standards. Any pleasure in success is always tempered by the fear that one might not be able to do it again. There is also the need to operate within the market – a necessary and significant consideration, for how else do works created in the seclusion of the studio reach a public?

In recent years, successful lectures in the UK and Australia have helped enormously to reach a wider public, as having the continuing exhibitions of her work, especially the *Stations of the Cross* paintings. But sympathetic intermediaries, dealers and gallerists are crucial. A turning point for Ghislaine's reputation with collectors in the North-West was the development of a strong working relationship with Martin Heaps and Martin Regan and with meeting artist and curator, Lesley Sutton. More recently she has enjoyed the support of a number of other gallerists including Chris and Julie McCabe and Dave O'Shea. Ghislaine is also proud to keep a close connection with our local community, she has shown at the Laughing Badger Gallery in Padfield and with Michael enjoys a close involvement with Glossop's classical music festival and a number of locally based charities.[38]

The PassionArt Trail
In 2014 Lesley Sutton initiated and organised with extraordinary flair a series of exhibitions that set a number of contemporary artists' works in six iconic Manchester buildings. These exhibitions were linked together as a sequence of meditative experiences and were given the title 'The PassionArt Trail' and organised to take place during Lent and Easter. It was conceived to offer a spiritual experience that would transcend the particularities of any one faith group.

Ghislaine's venue was the elegant eighteenth-century church of Saint Ann's in the centre of Manchester. It is a place where anyone can find a space to be still, quiet and safe within the noise and bustle of the city. The themes of the trail were forgiveness and reconciliation. Ghislaine showed a number of works in the church, but decided to paint a large canvas specifically for the occasion, to be set against the altar wall of the Lady Chapel. She chose as her subject, the *Return of the Prodigal Son*. Aware of the magisterial canvas by Rembrandt, she had set herself a serious challenge. Our good friend Jem Waygood and his son Jack agreed to act as models and accordingly the painting got underway in a fevered rush of concentrated activity. After innumerable studies the final painting was completed just in time for the opening of the exhibition. It depicts the moment of the meeting as the son falls to his knees and the father cradles his son's head in his enfolding embrace. Parallels with Ghislaine's earlier works became evident, the *Visitation Altarpiece* for example and the

The Corridor
1993
Oil on flax
152.4 x 182.9 cm
Collection of the Artist

Pregnant Self-Portrait
(opposite)
1987
Charcoal on paper
75.8 x 55.9 cm
Collection of the Whitworth Art
Gallery, Manchester
© Whitworth Art Gallery

painting of myself hugging Max as a baby and even Robin embracing him as a teenager in the Saint Anthony panel.

The British Museum Exhibition – Ice Age Art: Arrival Of The Modern Mind

'In my end is my beginning'. These famous lines from T. S. Eliot's late poems, 'The Four Quartets' seem apposite as we consider what lies ahead. We don't know. But it is fitting to close this biographical sketch with a drawing Ghislaine made of herself in 1987, when pregnant with Cordelia. She shows herself naked, hand on belly gazing into the studio mirror, but now, of course, she seems to look out of the picture, past the viewer into the far distance. It is a drawing of great expressive power that captures a sense of uncertainty and apprehension attendant upon her condition. But there is also in her look and the handling of the pigment, a fierce pride in the acceptance of impending motherhood. A drawing, quite literally, pregnant with the future.

Individual works may stand alone, but when set within Ghislaine's oeuvre, certain themes and recurring motifs become evident. Foremost amongst them, a respect for life and death in all its many aspects and the never-ending enigma of the identity of the self. All such visual and thematic connections create a powerful linkage between her early and late work. This drawing was seen some years later by Jill Cook, curator of Prehistory at the British Museum, when it was exhibited at the Whitworth Art Gallery in 1997. Unknown to us she saw the drawing and was determined to use it sometime in one of her own exhibitions. This came about in 2013 when she curated the groundbreaking exhibition, 'Ice Age Art: the Arrival of the Modern Mind'. Shown alongside works by Matisse, Picasso, Giacometti and Henry Moore, Ghislaine's drawing was exhibited in the first room adjacent to a group of small sculptures made around 30,000 years ago – amongst the first artefacts made by humans. They are images of women, probably crafted by women, representing women who are pregnant or who bear the marks on their bodies of having been so. Just another link in the chain.

As we read over this text it has become more and more evident that Ghislaine's art springs from her own life experience. Looking back on what we have written, we realise that, however hard one might try to give an insight into an artist's life, certain things remain difficult to put into words. Where are the days when Ghislaine felt that she would never paint again? The days when painting itself seemed an unnecessary and unwanted activity? Why continue the messy ragged practice of making art at all? And the answer? Maybe Philip Larkin said it best; when asked the same questions, he answered quite simply:

'to preserve things I have thought/seen/felt ... both for myself and others, which I am trying to keep from oblivion for its own sake'.[39]

The Return of the Prodigal Son
(detail)
2014
Acrylic on canvas
Collection of the Artist

1

The Corridor
(study)
1993
Charcoal on lining paper
55.9 x 94 cm (irregular)
Collection of the Artist

The Signature of Touch
The magic of line and the alchemy of paint

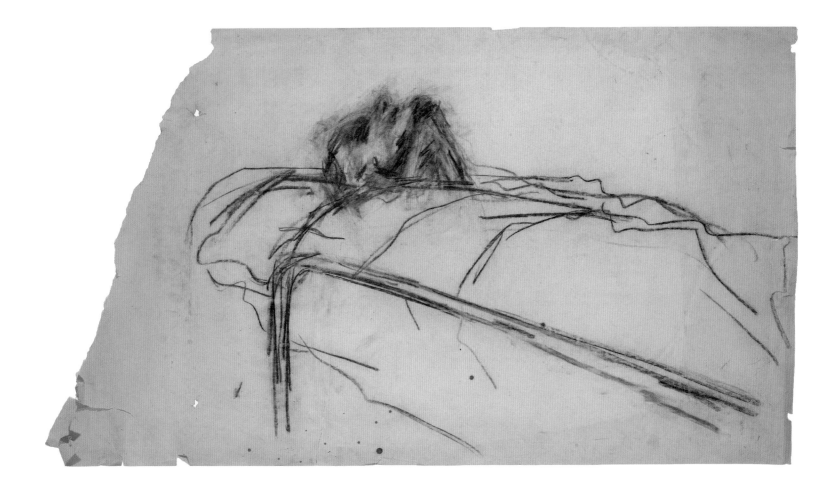

'In some pictures you can see, for example, that an arm has been in two or more different positions, and very often I'll leave that because I'm happy for a record of the making of the picture, traces of movement, to be left'.

Ghislaine Howard

I am a writer and so I write. But as I do so, I keep in mind my headmaster's immortal words to an auditorium crowded with disrespectful and noisy schoolboys: 'Every time I open my mouth some fool speaks,' he said. The ambiguous nature of this utterance never fails to remind me of the sometimes unforeseen consequences of language. Why can't paintings be left alone to speak for themselves? Words can obscure as well as illuminate. In the end, as Lowry said, it's the work that counts: the palpable actuality of paint on canvas and not the notoriously untrustworthiness of memory, anecdote or interpretation.

Ghislaine gave me a wry smile as she read the above. For like most artists she regards technique as something that you do rather than something you talk or write about. Hamlet would have agreed, perhaps: 'I have that within which passeth show ... You would pluck out the heart of my mystery'.[40] However, I feel that an appreciation of Ghislaine's working methods will not exhaust the mystery, but will only enrich it.

Ghislaine relishes the hard-won textured surfaces that charcoal on rough paper and oil paint can give – working the paper or canvas until it has a richness and variety that corresponds with the thing seen, the thing felt. To evoke not just the appearance of the natural world but its energies, its 'being'. She sees each new painting as a new adventure, one that tests the limits and capabilities of her painterly means. Her practice is nurtured, sustained and challenged by her visual engagement with the world and

her study of the work and methods of other artists. She works to no set formula, agreeing with Goya that, 'there are no rules in painting'.[41]

Each artist searches for their own means of expression and Ghislaine is no exception. Her paintings are instantly recognisable, not by a fixed style, but by what critic and art historian Richard Kendall called in reference to her work, 'the signature of touch'. So her technique and means of expression remain in a state of constant development.

In any one of her working spaces, canvases are to be seen, stacked everywhere. Gradually they encroach into the room until a necessary cull is called for – simply to allow her room to move. But any victory is only provisional, and the canvases creep back, for Ghislaine likes to work on several paintings at once, encouraging a familial relationship to develop amongst individual works, so that she can listen (eavesdrop might be a better word) to the conversations that occur between older works and those just completed or in progress. And, as in a real family, they give reassurance or unease in equal measure as unexpected parallels and challenges become apparent.

Looking through her work, it is evident that a number of stylistic traits have remained constant; her predilection for assertive brushwork is immediately apparent, though even this can change according to the needs of her subject matter. Her brushwork can, on occasion, become

Encrusted Palette with Knife and Spoon

After Caravaggio's Seven Works of Mercy (1607)
(detail)
2014
Oil on canvas
Collect Art

soft and caressing, her normally strong colours, muted and pastel-like, enlivened with authoritative touches of raw, calligraphic colour or tone depending upon the nature of the work in hand. She has a preference for rich earth colours that she enjoys setting against other hues and she relishes the evocative qualities of the colour blue in all its infinite variety. In his letters, the poet Rilke wrote eloquently of the beauty and power of Cézanne's blues.[42] In this sonnet he catches the shock of colour in a hydrangea, finding in words the qualities that Ghislaine strives for in her paintings:

...suddenly some new blue makes itself seen
In just one blossom, and we discover
A blue delighting in the green.[43]

Ghislaine seeks to preserve a fluidity and immediacy in her drawing and painting from the sketches that capture her first thoughts, through to the final canvas. For her, painting is essentially drawing by another means and the structural underpinning of charcoal or pigment often remains evident, embedded within the completed painting's surface. Such effects have always been part of any artist's craft, as the Roman writer Pliny noted in AD 77:
'It is a very unusual and memorable fact that the last works of artists and their unfinished paintings ... are more admired than those which they finished, because in them are seen the preliminary drawings left visible and the artists' actual thoughts.'[44]

As true today as it was then. Consider the 'unfinished' and late works of artists as various as Leonardo, Rembrandt, Cézanne, Degas, Bonnard, Picasso, Bacon and Auerbach. All artists whose working methods leave evidence in the very facture of the canvas of the concentrated efforts of eye, mind and hand working together with a recalcitrant material to make the work of art and in the process allowing the viewer a glimpse into the creative process itself.

In an interview with Philip Vann, given in October 1992, Ghislaine gave a vivid account of her working methods:

I do very many life drawings, studies from the human figure, which is the backbone of my art. Even though some of my paintings of parenthood are very big and monumental, I do not lose the sense of the particular, of intimacy and tenderness, little details like the tiny hand being held in the big adult hand, or the interplay between the feet of the mother and of those of the new child.

I don't find pencil sympathetic to work with. I use scene painter's charcoal, and broad decorators' brushes, made from hog hair. For me, painting is a

After Rembrandt's
The Three Crosses
(detail)
2001
Acrylic on canvas
Collection of the Artist

'Ghislaine Howard is a figurative artist who finds such passionate excitement in the abstract glories of colour and light that the well-worn distinction seems pointless. Her images work on both levels with equal power: we are swept away by the beauty of the actual paint even before we start to take delight in the image that she is celebrating.'

Sister Wendy Beckett, Women Critics Choose Women Painters, Bruton Street Gallery, 1992

very physical process. I like using the whole arm, putting my whole self into it. I like best very coarse, heavy flax canvas, which I stretch and size.

Initially in a painting, I draw in the simple shapes, the basic structure, with rapid movements, add fairly thin washes of paint, then rework the charcoal into the paint. Next, I start to apply thicker paint in areas that seem to be the mainspring of the composition, pivots in the structural scaffolding, like here, the shoulder, there, the neck. I use a palette knife to scrape off paint where need be, redefining all the time with charcoal.

There's no way I'm seeking a static, finished object. In some pictures you can see, for example, that an arm has been in two or more different positions, and very often I'll leave that because I'm happy for a record of the making of the picture, traces of movement, to be left. There is often a dialogue between the raw canvas and heavily worked areas. From underpainting, all sorts of colours come through.[45]

Ghislaine paints on a variety of supports, but normally on flax or linen canvas or wooden panels. This receiving surface is an active part of the painting process and is chosen for its particular qualities. Ghislaine chooses the surfaces she paints on with great care; panels offer a certain resistance to the pressure of the artist's hand, whereas a canvas support is a more responsive surface that answers each touch as the strings of a violin respond to the touch of its player. But again, there are no fixed rules and,

though she usually begins a painting on a mid-tone ground, one of her favourite surfaces is a canvas that has been begun and then, for whatever reason, abandoned. This often richly coloured and textured surface offers all kinds of unforeseen possibilities to the emerging painting that now claims its right to existence. Equally for Ghislaine, the bare canvas or underpainting is just another element in her pictorial repertoire to be used as required.

The Victorian art critic, John Ruskin, wrote in 1857 that, 'the whole value of what you are about, depends on colour. If the colour is wrong, everything is wrong: just as, if you are singing, and sing false notes, it does not matter how true your words are.'[46] Ghislaine would agree, she has her preferred colours, amongst them, cerulean blue, ultramarine, Naples yellow, yellow ochre, cadmium orange, Indian red and vermilion, colours that she often sets into certain favoured juxtapositions, indian reds against ultramarine, for example, or Naples yellow against cerulean blue. But her decisions are always intuitive as touches of colour are overlaid or set against each other. Though observed colour is significant for her, it is only a starting point that sets the painting in motion. As each colour is laid down, so it suggests others that excite or complement the developing structure of the painting, furthering its emotional impact.

Painting is both a physical and a mental activity, and as Ghislaine paints so she strives to achieve and sustain a sense of connectivity that allows

Self-Portrait, East Dene
(detail)
1983
Tempera on black paper
Collection of the Artist

The painting thereby becomes part of life,
not apart from it; not a pale shadow but a dynamic
equivalent for the experience of life.

her to 'inhabit' her chosen subject and the evolving painting at one and the same time. This demands a high level of concentration but it keeps the painting alive, so it follows that Ghislaine is happiest working in concentrated bursts of activity, punctuated by time spent in consideration of the next period of engagement or having a cup of tea.

Ghislaine establishes her basic compositional structures in a few broadly handled sketch-like strokes that retain something of the bodily movements that made them. These formative, exploratory strokes are then enriched by more delicate, but equally forceful, touches that serve to further define the subject, but also create a dynamic tension that in turn is enlivened by shifts of colour and tone.

Certain compositional elements reoccur that help the necessarily limited means of an artist to express what are, after all, the infinite complexities of the real. Drawings and preparatory work might help, but the real action takes place on the canvas. And that is something that, though planned, is also partly an unconscious activity. As the writer and psychologist Rudolf Arnheim wrote: 'All perceiving is also thinking, all reasoning is also intuition, all observation is also invention.'[47]

There is a logic to Ghislaine's compositions: each element works together and corresponds to the contained energies of her subject, whether a figure or a landscape. Each area of the painting plays with or against others, some are more intensely worked, to create moments of visual excitement or to emphasise a particular movement or point of tension. The adventure

of the picture's making is thereby left evident on the finished canvas – a lesson learnt from the improvisatory techniques of late Titian and Berthe Morisot. It is intriguing to imagine the artist as predator, who stalks her subject and then, paint brush in hand – pounces, pinning her quarry to the canvas, each subsequent strike economical and exact.

Each brushstroke builds on the next, plays its part in the construction of the whole, as a drystone waller sets each unique piece of stone into a wall, precisely into its allotted space. So, in painting, each decision adds something to the next, building up into a sequence of marks that endows the final image with a living, breathing quality that a bounding contour, carefully applied colour or delicate detailing might not give.

Ghislaine strives to keep these pictorial structures open, fluid. No part of the painting or drawing should be considered empty, but like the space it seeks to represent, it should be energised, to possess the same fullness of being as the world we inhabit. And, as the painting moves towards resolution, Ghislaine remains ever-critical, ready to scrape down, re-work as necessary in a constant pattern of revisions until the canvas is either achieved or destroyed. The painting thereby becomes part of life, not apart from it; not a pale shadow but a dynamic equivalent for the experience of life.

This said, within any successful painting there should also be a place to rest before moving on, a moment of quietude that serves to enhance the effect of the whole. It is the point that can pivot the painting into

**Naked Self-Portrait
Hotel Room**
(detail)
2011
Drypoint
Collection of the Artist

A drypoint is achieved by drawing directly into copper or perspex with a sharp point. Ink is spread across its surface, then carefully wiped away, so that it only remains in the furrows formed by the steel point cutting into the metal (or perspex). Depending on how much ink is removed from the surface so the resulting image, achieved by passing the plate through a printing press, is either more or less 'clean'. Ghislaine has used this technique to suggest the lights and shadows of the hotel room, rendering the forms and atmosphere in a masterful shorthand.

meaning; as a phrase can in a piece of music or a poem. It may be a touch of colour, a particular mark or series of marks or just a revealed area of empty canvas or paper. Such moments operate as punctuation points in a sentence or as Ghislaine once said to me, the readiness felt before leaping into the turning skipping rope.

I do not know which to prefer,
The beauty of inflections
Or the beauty of innuendoes,
The blackbird whistling
Or just after. [48]

Wallace Stevens's finely tuned poems catch something of this idea – to catch the beat of the wing of the angel (or blackbird), and the difficulty of doing so. As Monet reflected, *'You must know I'm entirely absorbed in my work. These landscapes of water and reflections have become an*

obsession. It's quite beyond my powers at my age, and yet I want to succeed in expressing what I feel, I've destroyed some … and I hope that something will come out of so much effort.' [49]

So, the fascination with what is difficult remains constant, and why not? To struggle with the paradoxical nature of art, in order to tell or show something of the reality of life and the world, through artifice. To get it right.

2

A Shared Experience
Beginnings

Ghislaine's interest in the themes of pregnancy and parenthood came into being when she became pregnant for the first time and began to make drawings of herself. Both Ghislaine and Professor David Peters Corbett have written eloquently about this aspect of her art and so I have left their words to speak for themselves.

Being a painter whose work springs from my own experience, my pregnancy presented a challenge that I could not ignore without denying the central basis of my inspiration. This challenge was the pictorial representation of the pregnant figure and to record and interpret my own pregnancy and subsequent motherhood.

Most representations of these subjects have been fashioned by male artists and, however sympathetic their treatment, they are seen inevitably from a male point of view. It seemed to me that here was an opportunity to create pictures that would not simply be a charting of the physical changes taking place, but would also express something about the psychological and emotional aspects of pregnancy.

As I looked around for images of pregnancy to compare with those that I was making, I was surprised to find just how few there were.

I worked directly from my own image, making a series of large drawings, and with each one I became aware of a new sense of urgency, perhaps due

to the lack of time, but more, I feel, because of the direct confrontation that self-portraiture involves .... As my pregnancy developed I found standing poses increasingly uncomfortable and so, partly for practical reasons, I decided to work from a seated position. Study for Self-Portrait, July 1984, is among the first of these. The figure dominates the composition, facing the viewer directly. The pose, which in earlier drawings is upright and alert with both hands on the knees, has now sunk into a relaxed and weary attitude. One hand supports the head and the gaze, whilst being directed outwards, fails to engage completely with the viewer, suggesting a preoccupation with the self.

After some more intensely worked drawings, I felt that I was now moving in the direction I wanted. The lines were stronger, more expressive of the form and, most of all, contained a real sense of heaviness, weight and fullness. On an emotional level I was beginning to catch the sense of repose and expectancy – that kind of anxious passive expectancy felt by the all-night traveller, alone in the small hours, waiting in some deserted station.[50]

And so as an artist whose work is concentrated on her own experiences, it was natural that she should chart not only her pregnancies, but also the development of our immediate family. In 1991 Ghislaine sent a proposal to Manchester Art Gallery for a project that would chart the beginnings and endings of life. After much consideration it was agreed that the scope of her engagement and the resulting exhibition should deal only with the

'On an emotional level I was beginning to catch the sense of repose and expectancy – that kind of anxious passive expectancy felt by the all-night traveller, alone in the small hours, waiting in some deserted station.'

Ghislaine Howard

**Midwife Waiting to Receive
the New Child**
(opposite)
1993
Oil on flax
119.4 x 119.4 cm
Collection of the Artist

**Study for Pregnant
Self-Portrait Standing**
1984
Charcoal and Conté on paper
76.2 x 53.4 cm
Collection of the Artist

Pregnant Self-Portrait
Seated in the Studio
1984
Charcoal and Conté on paper
76.2 x 53.4 cm
Private Collection

Mother with her New Child
(detail)
1993
Oil on canvas
Collection of the Artist

'Immediately after the birth of my own two children I realised the irony that I, the mother, was the only one of those present not to have witnessed the event'.

Ghislaine Howard

themes of pregnancy and hospital birth. For, although there are many images of scenes of childbirth in western art, mostly Nativities, there are very few which refer to the actuality of how babies are born. As Ghislaine remembers:

Immediately after the birth of my own two children I realised the irony that I, the mother, was the only one of those present not to have witnessed the event.

So in October 1992, Ghislaine returned to Saint Mary's Maternity Unit where her own children had been born, to work on a four-month residency that would culminate in a one–person show at Manchester Art Gallery in 1993, entitled, 'A Shared Experience'.

For a period of four months or so, two or three days each week, Ghislaine talked, sketched and listened to the women at Saint's Mary's, making small charcoal drawings. Back in the studio, these became the basis for larger, more resolved charcoal drawings and painted studies on paper which in turn informed the final oil paintings. As she worked, the paintings took on a particular colouristic character and a certain sense of gravitas. Ghislaine worked quickly on each one, painting, over-painting, drawing and repainting at speed, echoing the urgency of the birth process itself.

The following extracts from the journal that Ghislaine kept during the residency give a vivid picture of her experience and complement the emotional content and sense of empathy that is found in the resulting work:

Ghislaine's Journal

October 1

My daughter was born here five years ago, so I arrive for my first day as artist-in-residence with mixed feelings of familiarity and displacement. There is the same walk to the doors of the antenatal clinic, the same queue of women waiting. The maternity unit is an extraordinary institution: it is here the experience takes place that we have all shared – our naked entry into the world.

I talk to some women in the corridor waiting to be seen by midwives and doctors, but these initial approaches are very difficult. If I am to work with any expectant mother she must sign a consent form, which instantly formalises everything.

Most women immediately anticipate an invasion of their privacy and look away. I approach a young woman and her partner. She smiles, so I sit down and explain who I am. It is her first visit and she agrees to allow me through with her. She is nervous and her English is not very good. The

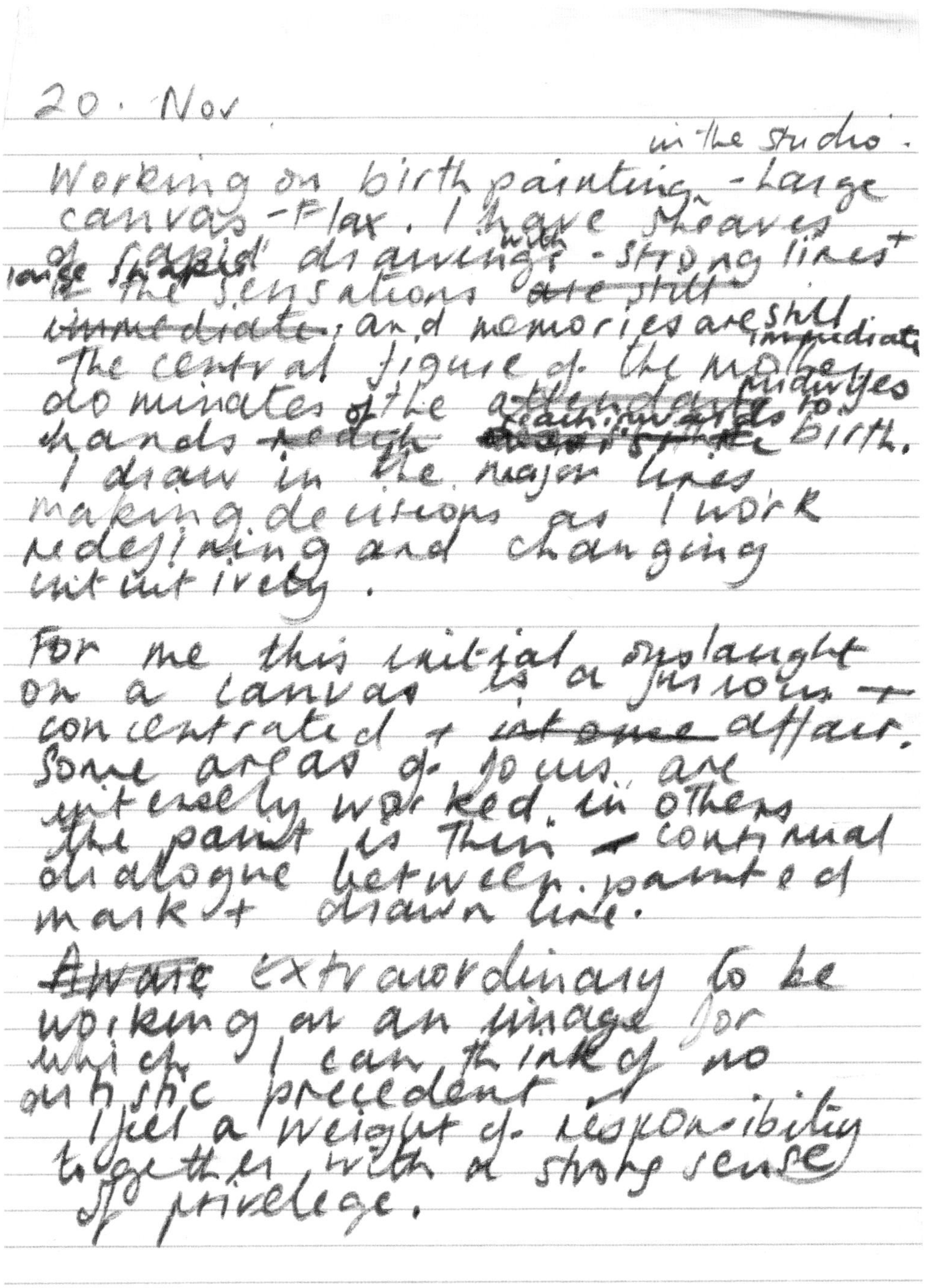

20. Nov

in the studio.

Working on birth painting - large
canvas - Flax. I have shoaves
~~large shapes~~ of ~~rapid~~ drawings with - strong lines+
~~& the sensations are still~~
~~immediate;~~ and memories are still immediate
The central figure of the m~~other~~ who yes
dominates the ~~attention~~ ~~giving~~ ~~drawing~~ minutes to
hands ~~redge~~ ~~moment of the~~ birth.
I draw in the major lines
making decisions as I work
redefining and changing
intuitively.

For me this initial onslaught
on a canvas is a furious +
concentrated + ~~intense~~ affair.
Some areas of focus are
intensely worked in others
the paint is thin - continual
dialogue between painted
mark + drawn line.

~~Aware~~ extraordinary to be
working on an image for
which I can think of no
artistic precedent +
I feel a weight of responsibility
together with a strong sense
of privelege.

She is having twins.

22 October
I've planned to be at D.B's caesarian tomorrow morning -I have talked to the consultant anaesthetist and consultant and all is O.K.

I feel exhilarated, nervous, excited and privileged to share their experience -also scared stiff that I might faint or cause a commotion which no-one has any time for.

We arrive in the preparation room on C.D.U. *Core Delivery Unit* D.B sits on the bed and as the anaesthetist explains procedures the room fills with people -there is a *new* anaesthetist who appears a little uneasy about my presence -suspicious, and I feel anxious, but immediately start to draw and take photographs -The only way I can cope with and make sense of what is happening.

I make quick, instinctive decisions, to get as near as possible to the table, to try to get behind D.B's head to see something of her viewpoint. To see the incisions, etc., would mean I would have to stand at a certain distance, and I would be like one of the observing students - and perhaps running the risk of letting a voyeuristic element creep into my work.
What I want to re-create is the experience as it is for the woman and her partner, what she sees when her baby is held up for the first time for her to see.

_____ . As if part of some arcane ritual, the robed figures move constantly in foreground and background, each knowing their job. Half my energy is spent *Find* keeping out of their way. Feel elated/ at being part of this professional team. I feel so strongly the sense of the moment, _____ ectancy and the high seriousness of every

Once she is on the table, things start to move very quickly and my rapid drawings become even more notational. I am tense, I don't want to miss a thing -in between jotting I take shots, camera indispensable

25 October
The work in the Studio is beginning to t -sudden thin wail and the first/ on some large drawings of the _____ dark back -white child is held for the mother to see -bloody, arms flailing so I'm working screwed up against the glare of the theatre lights [fro whilst the expe: security and company into bright, glaring separateness] *Stretching taut*

sense of urgency. Have to keep reassuring myself that I don't, I'm painting with a strong have to do everything immediately!

4 NOV IN S.C.B.U I draw a baby girl in her incubator, she lies on her front face to one side and adhesive patch to secure her feeding tubes, etc. her vest hangs loosely on her tiny form; the arm holes seem enormous -sticklike arm and legs splay out' relaxed in sleep [contrast between soft organic forms and rigid plastic structures and shapes. One tiny foot is arched, but toes curved on white mattress. The skin is reddish pink, but so soft and translucent. Note network of tiny veins beneath the surface. Draw mother holding her baby, and then move into the background as doctors and students come in for the ward rounds,

20.NOV.

**Pregnant Woman Sleeping
on the Ward**
(previous page)
1993
Oil on canvas
61 x 101.6 cm
Collection of the Artist

doctor is pleasant but brisk – not an easy atmosphere; I must learn to make relationships with both sides. A few rapid drawings of the examination result. This first contact reveals in a very clear way the scale of the task ahead.

October 2

Going to the hospital shop I meet E – she has had her baby and I go up to the ward with her. She is easy with me and her child, a beautiful, smooth, brown baby, is sleepy with jaundice. We talk and I make drawings as she feeds her child. I am finding that the problems of fitting into this huge institution resolve themselves through contact with individuals.

Draw and photograph JE, who is a little uneasy at first. Very dark skin, hair drawn back, heavily laden body, she wears a mint-green dressing gown of thin material which falls and enfolds her huge body eloquently. Her pose is archetypal. She has three weeks to wait here and constantly worries about her family back home.

October 4

I start to look at the drawings and photographs I've taken and begin to focus on the hands and the atmosphere of intense concentration and

professionalism that pervades the hospital – hands, arms and backs are as expressive as faces.

October 7

I have been working on some small paintings of E and her baby from the sketches I made earlier. They are tender and intimate. Mothers and children do fall into the clichéd poses of art history as much as they do unusual ones. Still focusing closely on hands and child. How immersed one can become in contemplation of these tiny creatures.

I arrive in the preparation room of the delivery unit where D is having twins by caesarean section. The doctors and D have consented to my presence and I feel exhilarated and also scared stiff that I might faint. As soon as the anaesthetist, who is slightly suspicious of me, starts to work, I begin to draw, which is the only way I can cope with and make sense of what is happening. I make quick, instinctive decisions: to get as near as possible to the table, to try to get behind D's head to see something of her viewpoint. What I need to recreate is the experience as it is for the woman and her partner, what she sees when her baby is held up for the first time.

As things commence, my rapid drawings become ever more notational. A nurse is in attendance, like a figure from Giotto, arms outstretched, waiting

Antenatal Examination
(opposite left)
1992
Oil on canvas
76.2 x 91.4 cm
Collection of the Artist

Dressing the New Child
(opposite right)
1992
Oil on canvas
35.5 x 45.7 cm
Collection of the Artist

'It is extraordinary to be working on an image for which I can think of no artistic precedent and I feel a weight of responsibility together with a strong sense of privilege'.
Ghislaine Howard

to receive the child into a green cloth. Despite the bright light, my own sense of the colours is formed by the tones of the flesh and the green robes of the medical staff. A truly uplifting experience.

October 25

The work in the studio is beginning to take off. I've worked on some large drawings of the caesarean preliminaries. My mind is buzzing with images, so I'm working on large rapid, inky watercolours whilst the experience is fresh. I am painting with a strong sense of urgency.

October 26

Working on a birth painting in the studio, I have sheaves of rapid drawings with strong lines and large shapes. The sensations and memories are still immediate. The central figure of the woman dominates, the hands of the attendants reach inwards towards the centre of the painting. I draw in the major lines with scene painters charcoal, making decisions as I work and changing things intuitively. For me, this initial onslaught on the canvas is a furious and concentrated affair – some areas of focus are intensely worked, in others the paint is thin.

I am trying to concentrate on the sense of human drama that I am experiencing in the hospital and focus on the expressive potential of the human body. It is extraordinary to be working on an image for which I can think of no artistic precedent and I feel a weight of responsibility together with a strong sense of privilege.[51]

The immediacy and forthrightness of Ghislaine's account is matched by the thoughtful and sensitive response of David Peters Corbett, a friend and fellow art historian, who wrote the following in the catalogue that accompanied the exhibitions of the work at Manchester Art Gallery and the Wellcome Foundation in London:

'The residency, which was the first of its kind, gave her a unique opportunity to observe and record the work of a busy maternity unit. The result is a powerful series of works in several media which describe the experience of hospital birth with an illuminating visual intelligence and an unsentimental compassion that includes the medical teams and the partners as well as the mothers and babies.

'Howard shows us the medical staff embedded in the circumstances of the delivery. The faces we can read are intent, the hands that figure repeatedly in the pictures are competent, professional, steady, but also, as in the painting of the midwife palpating the mother or the doctor caring for a baby in the incubator, they are gentle. The hands that reach into the painting from all sides in the central birth scene are entirely confident in the job they are doing, but also tender, sympathetic. They are enabling, not forcing, the birth.

'There is an interplay between the expressions that can be read out of the smudged, apparently rapid notation, and the non-expressions of all those faces turned away or shielded from us: faces concealed by the surgical mask, by an embrace or by the medical personnel who cluster round, obscured by a preoccupation which seems to exclude us (with a job of work to be done, with the baby in the mother's arms), or cut off by the picture frame or by unconsciousness.

'In the one painting where there might be a direct meeting of glances between the spectator and the subject, the woman seems entirely separate within the privacy of her experience and her face is obscured by the oxygen mask strapped over nose and mouth.

'Ghislaine Howard's work exhibited here is about a subject that art has not dealt with before, the nature of hospital birth. It is a powerful and compelling achievement.[52]

One of the most innovative aspects of the exhibition was the fact that it ever took place at all. The exhibition was the first of its kind and situated as it was within a prestigious City Art Gallery, it could not but operate as a subversive counterpart to the masculine view of the world that is so much in evidence in its permanent collection.[53] And for at least one person, the forthrightness of Ghislaine's painterly response was simply too shocking for words. We remember standing in the doorway of the exhibition space and seeing a woman entering the gallery with a companion. On the opposite wall was the most explicit of the birth paintings. We watched as she walked towards it, talking in a loud voice of how effectively the reds and greens worked together. Perhaps she assumed

that what she was moving towards was an abstract painting, for as the precise nature of the image became apparent, she stopped in her tracks and taking her friend by the arm, we heard her say, 'No, no, oh no!' as she made her way towards the safety of the Victorian rooms above. Happily, this incident was the exception rather than the rule and the majority of comments were overwhelmingly positive.

Couple During Labour
(study)
1993,
Pencil on paper
12.7 x 17.8 cm
Collection of the Artist

Couple During Labour
(opposite)
1993
Oil on canvas
91.4 x 91.4 cm
Collection of the Artist

'The drama of natural childbirth is juxtaposed with the fearful mysteries of the Caesarian operation.' The comments from the Mancunian audience, registered in the visitors' book, show a striking lack of embarrassment, either with the gynaecological frankness or the emotional transparency of the work ... deeply felt and compassionately executed; 'the artist has dared not to distance herself.'

Joan Crossley, Women's Art Journal, July 1993

Caesarian Birth
1993
Oil on flax
91.4 x 91.4 cm
Collection of the Artist

Mother Reaching Towards her New Child
(opposite)
1993
Oil on flax
182.9 x 116.8 cm
Collection of the Artist

Birth Painting
1993
Oil on flax
121.9 x 152.4 cm
Collection of the Artist

Moments after Birth
(opposite)
1993
Oil on canvas
121.9 x 121.9 cm
Collection of the Artist

Max: the First Day
1985
Oil on canvas
121.9 x 182.9 cm
Collection of the Artist

3

Josette in Rehearsal
1995
Charcoal on paper
40.7 x 30.5 cm
Collect Art

The Telling Gesture
The silent eloquence of the body

Ezra Pound once said that when it comes to poetry, 'only emotion endures'.[54] The artist Frank Auerbach would probably agree, only he put it somewhat differently, but no less precisely: 'Absolutely bloody everything feeds into my work. Someone can annoy you; the man at the corner shop does not say good morning. It all feeds in. I think it has to do with death. My childhood and biographical reasons – I think I must have felt that unless one justifies one's life and has something to show for it, then the whole thing is wasted.'[55]

We are transient beings moving through time and space, we meet people and interact with family members, friends or strangers, those we love and those we fear. Humans are performative creatures, we play roles depending on time and circumstance and our changing performances are of perennial fascination to us all and a compulsive subject of interest to artists and writers of all kinds.

To Catch Life on the Wing
Some things disappear almost immediately, others remain forever in our memories until they fade along with ourselves. Artists need to train their memories; it is the core of their practice – here is wise old Degas:

'It is much better to draw what you can't see any more but in your memory. It is a transformation in which imagination and memory work together. You only reproduce what struck you, that is to say the necessary.'[56]

Succinct and exact. Painters and writers are particularly aware of the fragility of memory and how it cradles our sense of who and what we are. For Ghislaine this is one of the most powerful impulses that keeps her painting, her ever-present awareness of time moving on and the inevitable separations that it brings. She is motivated by a need to catch hold of the moments that matter to her; a walk on the moors, watching our children learn to walk, her own image and those of her family and friends. In however limited a fashion, art is a means of keeping such memories forever and the artist's business is to catch the defining moment in the shifting gestures of a body or the subtleties of facial expression, the things that express or signal the complex emotions of the people around her. By centring her art on her own subjective response to the world she plays a game of subtle resistance to any idea that art should be impersonal or objective. Much of her work is physical and robust, operating as a form of embodiment, a way of linking with the stuff of the world. Not

Howard 1998

Acrobat
1996
Acrylic on panel
61 x 61 cm
Collection of the Artist

Humans are performative creatures, we play roles depending on time and circumstance and our changing performances are of perennial fascination to us all and a compulsive subject of interest to artists and writers of all kinds.

just a matter of looking, but as she says so often of 'feeling' – not in a sentimental way, but in a deep, fierce possessive understanding of the word, inscribing herself into the world as a teenager might in leaving their tag on a wall.

However, some of Ghislaine's paintings also possess a haunting, spectral quality, for they are reflections of someone once present, but now absent. This might well be one of the reasons why mirrors feature so largely in her work. For, like a mirror, a painting preserves traces of the past in the present: ghosts in fact. But, unlike a mirror, drawings and paintings preserve that 'other' forever, whereas a mirror can only preserve our image for as long as we stand before it.[57]

Family

Although the residency at Saint Mary's was time-consuming and physically and emotionally draining, it did not preclude Ghislaine from continuing to paint her own life. And so as ever, the two aspects of her art supported each other. This was a way of working that was to become Ghislaine's standard practice and has allowed her to invest her public works with a sense of intimacy and contrariwise, it has enabled her more intimate works to attain a certain gravitas that removes them from the sentimental or merely anecdotal.

Ghislaine had not forgotten that her original proposal to Manchester Art

Gallery included the plan to spend time recording and interpreting the end period of life, so in the months immediately following the 'Shared Experience' exhibition, she returned to the drawings that she had made at Shire Hill Hospital in Glossop and began to use these as the foundation for a number of ambitious canvases paralleling those that had been shown earlier in Manchester.

Ghislaine was gaining a reputation within the North-West as a sensitive painter of human lives and as a result she was asked in late 1993 by Risley Prison education office if she would undertake to work with a group of male inmates, to help them to create and exhibit a body of artwork responding to their situation as she in turn recorded her own response of prison life.

Having recently completed a similar project at Saint Mary's Maternity Unit in Manchester, I welcomed the opportunity to witness life at another institution. Like a hospital, a prison is an enclosed world, with its own codes of behaviour, in which a wide range of human situations are acted out.

My involvement with Risley allowed me to continue my interest in the depiction of the human figure, looking at ways in which the individual is affected by particular environments and experiences ... I did not go in search of overly dramatic situations, but rather allowed my day-to-day contact with individuals to suggest the subject matter for my work.

Circus Performer
2016
Acrylic on board
91.4 x 61 cm
Collection of the Artist

Carmella in Rehearsal
2003
Acrylic on board
30.5 x 22.8 cm
Collect Art

**Rehearsal Study, Women of
Troy, National Theatre**
1995
Acrylic on flax
50.8 x 45.7 cm
Collect Art

**Distraught Man
(Abreaction piece)**
1997
Oil on flax
61 x 76.2 cm
Collection of the Artist

When painting the theatre, like Degas, Ghislaine instinctively withdraws from depicting moments of high drama in favour of those just preceding the main event or those that immediately follow.

Actors

Ghislaine's eye for dramatic scenarios may be seen throughout her work. Her images of childbirth and prison life all depend upon the silent eloquence of the body. When such things are caught just right, then the viewer may experience the uneasy feeling that they are intruders watching someone's private life being played out or alternatively there may be a sense of recognition, of becoming an invisible guest within the scene depicted.

When painting the theatre, like Degas, Ghislaine instinctively withdraws from depicting moments of high drama in favour of those just preceding the main event or those that immediately follow. For example, when two actors collapse into each other's arms at the end of a strenuous rehearsal, the release of tension and the overflow of emotion make an irresistible subject. She is also attracted to that moment between movements that often reveals more than the completed action itself. Again, something learnt from Degas as much as from direct observation.

Women's Refuge

Whilst walking in a local park, Ghislaine struck up a conversation with a young boy who had stopped to stroke our dog. He told her that he had just moved to the town and he and his mum were living 'at the Refuge'. This meeting coincided with an initiative from the Arts Council inviting artists to submit proposals for 'residencies in unusual places'. Struck by the idea that right in the heart of Glossop there was a place of safety for those escaping domestic violence, Ghislaine applied for and secured a placement to spend time there.

As before, Ghislaine kept a journal of her experiences:

At first glance, life seems fairly normal here, like any communal flat or house share, people sitting around watching television or making a cup of tea. But as you spend time and gain sensitivity to your circumstances, so you sense the tensions that lie just beneath the surface, as at Risley Prison and to some extent Saint Mary's, tensions that can erupt for good or ill at any moment – it's about atmosphere. Sometimes you can almost taste it and it is this as much as anything that I wished to express in these paintings. A simple act such as someone lifting a curtain or putting their child to bed within the safety of the Refuge suddenly becomes unutterably touching.

Such experiences taught Ghislaine a lot, not just about her own feelings, but also about the ways that art can help people to become more positive about themselves and their own lives. Both in the doing of it and by feeling that their own experiences were being recognised and valued by being depicted. So the women and children made their own responses to their situation through drawing and photography, whilst Ghislaine sought her own artistic response. The very restrictions of working in such places gave birth to some inspirational compositional and painterly ideas. For example, it was absolutely necessary that given the nature of the Refuge, the faces of the women and children could not be shown fully and as a consequence, Ghislaine became more sensitive to the silent eloquence of the body, the significance of ancillary details and the emotional possibilities of certain conjunctions of line and colour may suggest.

Josette Bushelungo as Cassandra

The Telling Gesture

The search for the telling gesture that took Leonardo da Vinci out into the marketplace takes Ghislaine to similar places, but also to those great repositories of humanity – the television and the computer screen. Actors on television, the stage or film know how to use their bodies and faces to great effect, and so, for example, the effectiveness of the pause button that catches an arbitrary moment or gesture can inspire her with all kinds of possibilities. She finds inspiration particularly from 1950s black-and-white films, Japanese and Chinese films or even soaps or detective dramas – the lighting, the *mise en scène*, the blurred movement of the main or subsidiary protagonists – all can be marvellous sources for invention – as of course are building sites! The easy play of bodies, professionals knowing exactly what they are meant to be doing, moving with grace, economy and a knowledge that is so important to the task in hand that it becomes almost unconscious. Hence Ghislaine's fascination with scaffolders, for example. Their poses so often remind her of the Passion or figures from Giorgione, or Raphael, those exemplars of balance, dynamism and grace. Other times they may suggest the energised bodies twisting into space found in the paintings of Tintoretto and Titian. So how could she resist stealing such images? One might thieve, all well and good, but one must also re-invent, re-imagine, re-create. When Ghislaine looks back to such figures from the past, she learns not just from what they painted, but also from what they didn't paint.

So, through such procedures, Ghislaine is able to weave together direct experience and borrowed images of all kinds, sifting them through the mechanism of sketches, studies and paintings to make visible what might otherwise remain invisible, giving access to unfamiliar worlds or showing the familiar world in a new way, not only expressing reality, but extending our understanding of it.

Josette as Cassandra
Women of Troy
National Theatre
1995
Pencil and charcoal on paper
35.5 x 25.4 cm
Collection of the Artist

It was absolutely necessary that given the nature of the Refuge, the faces of the women and children could not be shown fully and as a consequence, Ghislaine became more sensitive to the silent eloquence of the body, the significance of ancillary details and the emotional possibilities of certain conjunctions of line and colour may suggest.

Crouching Figure
1995
Oil on panel
30.5 x 22.8 cm
Collect Art

Leaving the Refuge
2000
Acrylic on canvas
101.6 x 127 cm
Collection of the Artist

**Rehearsal, Women of Troy
National Theatre**
1995
Acrylic on canvas
40.7 x 45.7 cm
Courtesy of Gateway Gallery

Actors Embracing (Blue)
2015
Acrylic on board
30.5 x 22.8 cm
Collection of the Artist

Embracing Couple
Piccadilly Station
2016
Acrylic and pigment on board
91.4 x 61 cm
Courtesy of Art Decor Gallery

Embracing Couple (Red)
2015
Oil on board
30.5 x 22.8 cm
Collection of the Artist

Actor with Outstretched
Arms
(overleaf)
1995
Acrylic on flax
101.6 x 182.9 cm
Collection of the Artist

Rugby Player
(opposite)
2015
Oil on linen
50.8 x 40.7 cm
Collect Art

Skateboarder
(study)
2014
Oil on board
30.5 x 22.8 cm
Collect Art

Skateboarder
2014
Oil on board
91.4 x 61 cm
Collect Art

Tattooed Man, Risley
1994
Oil on canvas
88.9 x 73.7 cm
Collection of the Artist

Segregation Unit, Risley
(study)
1994
Oil on panel
24.4 x 28 cm
Collect Art

Segregation Unit, Risley
1994
Oil on flax
119.5 x 119.5 cm
Courtesy of Gateway Gallery

Behold the Man
(study for the first *Station*)
Oil on linen
127 x 101.6 cm
Collection of the Artist

4

Religious Commissions
Paintings for sacred spaces

The narrowness of the gap that separates us from our fellow animals is something that has fascinated many artists that Ghislaine admires: Rembrandt, Goya, Degas, Picasso and Bacon. She recognises their unflinching acceptance of our bestial natures that renders our aspirations to be something other, all the more poignant. This is a powerful undercurrent that runs deep within her work and it is one of the reasons why she is drawn to religious subject matter – the great stories, as we would see them. Being brought up in the Christian faith, Ghislaine considers Christ to be, as the work of Rembrandt and van Gogh seem to suggest, deeply human.

Religion played an important role in Ghislaine's family and in her early imaginative life. Her mother and father were both regular churchgoers and so the family was expected to follow suit. As she grew up, so Ghislaine's relationship with the Catholic Church became more problematic. Going to Catholic schools, she soon developed a healthy disregard for the darker side of religion, not least after being told repeatedly as a young child by one of her teachers, Mother Martina (she remembers all their names so clearly) that if she didn't behave herself, then the Devil would be waiting at the foot of the bed to pinch her toes. Stern stuff for a six-year-old.[58] Arthur Rimbaud, the most revolutionary of nineteenth–century poets, put it succinctly, when he wrote that one is always a slave to one's baptism. It may prove impossible to break those chains completely, but at least we can give them a good rattle. For both

of us, the experience of our churchgoing days has given us the means to develop a profound, if complex, relationship with the ideas and great works connected with the Christian faith, be it music, art, literature or architecture. It is part of the fabric of our lives. So in Ghislaine's more ambitious works there is the definite ambition to create a synthesis or rapport between the sacred and the secular. This ambition is evident in all Ghislaine's work relating to religious themes, which include the *Visitation Altarpiece* at Liverpool Hope University, the *Saint Anthony Sequence* for a stately home in North Yorkshire and the *Washing of the Feet* for the Methodist Modern Art Collection. But the largest undertaking was the *Stations of the Cross / The Captive Figure* for Liverpool Cathedral.

I'm sure every artist has somewhere in the back of their minds the first painting that made an impact upon them. There might be many contenders, but for Ghislaine, her childhood was shadowed by the presence of church art – the stained glass windows and statues but above all, the gaudy, mass-produced *Stations of the Cross* that punctuated the architecture of her local church, Saint Mary's in Eccles. She remembers the flaking paint work of this cavernous space and each year, just before Christmas, how one of the side chapels was transformed into a massive craggy overhang in which, lit by candlelight, was the Nativity, straw, baby, kings and shepherds; all shabby and makeshift, but completely magical to a small child.

Work in progress
Trinity Chapel
Liverpool Hope University
2003

Ghislaine remembers:

Such visceral experiences, together with the language, music and ritual of the church became the context for her future encounters with the great paintings of the European tradition. For both of us the great works of art of the Christian canon could never be just 'great', 'important' or 'beautiful' works of art. Rather, they act as fields of contention, attempts to reach beyond the merely formal into the world of human actions, desires and anxieties. Embedded within them are stories, symbols and rituals. Who can tell what effects such things have upon the developing imagination of young children? And how can one assess the extent to which they have formed one's emotional and creative life?

As I grew older, I came into contact with more emotionally charged versions of Christ's Passion than the ones familiar to me from school and my local church. Especially significant to me were those single episodes such as Rubens's great Deposition and the resonant image of the Entombment

paintings of Titian and Poussin in the National Gallery of Ireland. It became my ambition to continue that tradition, by putting some of the emotive power of such images into a suite of works corresponding to the 14 Stations of the Cross. I had been considering this ambition for some time and over a period of five years I produced a large body of drawings and studies.

And from that private impulse came Ghislaine's first religious commission from Liverpool Hope University to paint 14 large canvases for Liverpool Cathedral as part of their millennium celebrations.

In her student days, Ghislaine had been interested primarily in a work's formal and expressive qualities; awareness of any religious content remained dormant. It was only when she had the idea of revisiting the *Stations*, that those images that had seared themselves upon her imagination as a child, that the universal relevance of this great story became more and more evident. From as early as 1992 Ghislaine had been

How barren the world would be without the stories,
art and buildings connected with such ideas.

The Empty Tomb
In the crypt at York Minster
2012

'Like all good sacred art Howard's derives its strength not from a vague, disembodied religious feeling but from a visceral sympathy with the human condition, expressed through the primal medium of paint.'

Laura Gascoigne, The Tablet

fascinated by the challenge of reinterpreting these time-honoured images which present a veritable choreography of movement, expressing passion, pathos and violence. All religious institutions are profoundly human and none are untouched by barbarity, but how barren the world would be without the stories, art and buildings connected with such ideas.

Our friend, Chris Ackroyd, an art historian and life model, agreed to pose for the figure of Christ and over the next few years regular drawing sessions took place in the Glossop studio. Before each session, we would discuss the relevant texts so that Chris could immerse himself in the narrative, much as an actor might. As he moved through the key moments of the Biblical story, so Ghislaine drew and re-drew at speed as if she were a witness responding to the drama passing before her eyes. It is fascinating to consider that these drawings began almost immediately after Ghislaine had completed her residency at Saint Mary's Maternity Unit and at the very time of her Risley and Women's Refuge projects.

Strangely, I felt strong parallels between what I was witnessing in the maternity unit with women in labour and the themes of the Stations of the Cross. The women were all on a journey from which there was no turning back, and though their experience was theirs and theirs alone, they were supported by an array of attendant figures.

Such experiences opened a door in her thinking about her art, suggesting the possible ways in which she could perhaps make an art that really

mattered – in however small or modest a fashion. We also recognised that by taking up this subject matter, she was unconsciously defining herself against what often seemed to us to be a cynical and superficial art world.

Work on the final sequence of paintings began in 1999, six years after the idea had first suggested itself. Ghislaine worked surrounded by her drawings, and the paintings evolved as she took the best out of each of the individual studies, the final canvases emerging, like Frenhofer's 'masterpiece', from an apparent chaos of swirling lines. Although I might have been thinking of Balzac's famous novella *The Unknown Masterpiece*,[59] Ghislaine was still reeling from seeing an exhibition of Jackson Pollock's paintings at the Tate, where one of his monochrome canvases had made a particularly strong impression upon her.

The finished works are painted in monochrome, 12 measuring 6' x 5', and the *Ecce Homo* and the *Deposition*, 8' x 6'. They were completed in a relatively short period of time and each one is a distillation of the numerous studies she had made directly from Chris, each preserving the immediacy of the original charcoal drawings. Those paintings that didn't work were over-painted or destroyed and a new version begun. Each was worked on in company with the others using acrylic mixed with sand and a PVA medium that gave the surface of each a robust sculptural quality. The use of black and white meant that each *Station* would be legible from a distance and respond to the ambient light that is one of the defining features of any cathedral.

Bound Figure
1997
Oil on linen
117 x 77 cm
Collection of the Artist

The Washing of the Feet
(top)
2004
Acrylic on canvas
101.6 x 127 cm
Methodist Modern Christian Art
Collection © TMCP
used with permission

Washing of the Feet
(study)
2004
Acrylic on board
61 x 91.4 cm
Collection of the Artist

Study for Jesus is Lowered into the Tomb
1999
Oil on canvas
152.4 x 182.9 cm
Private Collection

Sponsored by Liverpool Hope University and endorsed by Amnesty International, it was envisaged (and has come to pass) that the paintings would have a life of their own. Since then, they have travelled far and wide to cathedrals and other venues around the UK including Canterbury, Gloucester, Derby, Lichfield, Exeter and York Minster, Derby Art Gallery and elsewhere.

There are so many stories we could tell, so many poignant and appreciative comments from the various visitors' books, but one of the most memorable happenings was when we took one of the large monochrome studies into the Anglican Cathedral for the first time. Ghislaine had begun the project thinking in terms of colour and we brought the black-and-white painting into the nave to consider the size and impact of the composition within that vast space. As we set the canvas in place, leaning it precariously against a chair, we saw two vergers, robes flying, racing from the distance towards us. We immediately thought that we had transgressed in some way and anticipated a reprimand. But no – they were simply running to express their appreciation. As they drew near, they stopped and one said, 'That's great, that is. I could see it from right back there,' which confirmed Ghislaine's decision to keep the final works in monochrome and to keep as them as broadly painted as possible.

The key to the whole enterprise was centred upon the realisation that cathedrals reach out to a broad and ever-changing audience – people of all faiths and no faith, tourists, school parties, art lovers, those who enter in need of shelter, safety or simply to get out of the rain. In 2001, Helen Bamber of the Medical Foundation for the Care of Victims of Torture said at a special evening dedicated to the charity at Canterbury Cathedral: 'Ghislaine Howard's images are compelling, powerful, and emphatic. They are unusual in that they communicate man's inhumanity to man, to the art lover and lay person alike. These are very important paintings that transcend the limitations of the exhibition space to speak to us all.'[60]

In 2007, in anticipation of Liverpool's Year as the Capital of Culture, 2008, Liverpool Cathedral commissioned Ghislaine to paint a final piece that would complete the series and accordingly she produced a monumental canvas, *The Empty Tomb*.

'Like all good sacred art,' Laura Gascoigne, art critic for *The Tablet*, wrote of the completed sequence, 'Howard's derives its strength not from a vague, disembodied religious feeling but from a visceral sympathy with the human condition, expressed through the primal medium of paint.'

**Lamentation of the Women
of Jerusalem**
(opposite)
1999
Charcoal on paper
71 x 48 cm
Royal Collection Trust
© HER MAJESTY QUEEN
ELIZABETH II 2016

**Jesus Falls for the Second
Time**
1999
Oil on board
71 x 91.4cm
Collect Art

At a time when we're bombarded with graphic photographs of human suffering and degradation, paint still retains its power to give us pause – to demand from us an investment of time and energy in recognition of that invested by the artist. "My soul is very sorrowful, even unto death; remain here, and watch with me", Jesus begged in the Garden of Gethsemane. Howard has watched and walked with him on his last journey, stopping at each *Station* on the way; and the emotional and physical labour she has invested makes her audience want to stop and watch with her.'[61]

It was very special to see the sequence of the *Stations of the Cross / The Captive Figure* completed in such a satisfying and thought-provoking way, and it was breathtaking for the *Empty Tomb* to be set within the magnificent space of the crypt of York Minster whilst the Stations and *365* panels from the *365 Series* were on view above in the nave. For two years Ghislaine had worked closely with the Minster, her paintings being an integral part of their Year of Reconciliation activities. On the occasion of planning their first showing of the *Station* at Easter in 2011, Ghislaine suggested that she should produce a painting of Judas to accompany the exhibition.

As we were discussing the installation of the paintings in the magnificent spaces of the Minster, it occurred to me that in all this great narrative, one figure was absent. The one person without whom, the Easter story and all that followed would have been very different – Judas.

It was agreed and Ghislaine set to work on a number of possibilities. She soon rejected the dramatic images that she had been considering and decided to paint not a large oil, but a small panel, the same size as the *365* paintings – 8 x 6 inches: *Judas – the Departure*. The painting was delivered and became the focus of a special service held at the Minster on the first evening of the Lenten period, when the Dean, the Very Reverend Keith Jones, presented a meditation on the painting, after which the small panel was hidden away in a secret location within the building until the Easter celebrations when it was brought back into view as a symbol of forgiveness and reconciliation. It was then once again hidden away until the following Easter.

A commission for Ghislaine to paint a new series of the *Station* for the Minster was planned, using contemporary subject matter developed from the *365* paintings, but sadly this came to nought, although it may well have sown the seeds for the Seven Acts of Mercy project, something we were not aware of at the time.

'These significant and powerful works open up opportunities to highlight and explore the issue of torture and the plight of victims of oppression all over the world.'

Dan Jones, Amnesty International

Stations of the Cross / The Captive Figure

1 Jesus is Condemned to Death
1999
Acrylic and sand on canvas
244 x 183 cm
Collection of the Artist

2 Jesus Receives His Cross
2000
Acrylic and sand on canvas
183 x 142 cm
Collection of the Artist

3 Jesus Falls for the First Time
1999
Acrylic and sand on canvas
183 x 141 cm
Collection of the Artist

4 Jesus Meets His Mother
1999
Acrylic and sand on canvas
183 x 141 cm
Collection of the Artist

5 Simon of Cyrene Helps Jesus to Carry His Cross
2000
Acrylic and sand on canvas
183 x 142 cm
Collection of the Artist

6 Veronica Wipes the Face of Jesus
2000
Acrylic and sand on canvas
183 x 142 cm
Collection of the Artist

7 Jesus Falls for the Second Time
2000
Acrylic and sand on canvas
141 x 183 cm
Collection of the Artist

8 The Lamentation of the Women of Jerusalem
2000
Acrylic and sand on canvas
183 x 142 cm
Collection of the Artist

9 Jesus Falls for the Third Time
1999
Acrylic and sand on canvas
183 x 142 cm
Collection of the Artist

10 Jesus is Stripped of His Garments
2000
Acrylic and sand on canvas
183 x 142 cm
Collection of the Artist

11 Jesus is Nailed to the Cross
1999
Oil on Canvas
141 x 183 cm
Collection of the Artist

12 Jesus Dies on the Cross
1999,
Acrylic and sand on canvas
183 x 141 cm
Collection of the Artist

13 Jesus is Taken Down from the Cross
1999
Acrylic and sand on canvas
142 x 183 cm
Collection of the Artist

14 Jesus is Laid in the Tomb
2000
Acrylic and sand on canvas
244 x 183 cm
Collection of the Artist

There is something I have always aspired to do.
I would like to paint a Christ on the Cross...

What a symbol!

One could rack one's brains till the end of time
and never find anything like it to equal
the image of suffering.

That is the basis of humanity. That is its poetry.[62]

Edouard Manet

Judas: the Departure
2011
Oil on board
20.3 x 15.25 cm
Collection of the Artist

A meditation by the Very Reverend Keith Jones, Dean of York Minster, 2011

'The immediate impression is of black and white, but in fact there is a good deal of colour here, and beautiful colour too: a warm sand tint on Judas's neck, most noticeably on his hand; but it also occurs elsewhere, significantly in the background, where it adds a liveliness to the whiteness, and it also gives a hint that the trousers are rather deep brown rather than black. The richness of colour continues in the complex pattern of lemon on the back of his waistcoat which is at the centre of the picture. And then there is blue, a delicate and interesting blue, at its purest in the band along the base of the picture, but also infused into the shadow to the top right-hand of the painting.

'The figure itself is very upright, the horizontal line at the base emphasising the height of the man who is slim and vigorous in form. Ghislaine Howard is an artist who is always able to catch the way in which human weight is balanced in its daily movements, and it can be seen here in the way the legs are braced for the action with the coat. The action is quite slow, definite, but preoccupied. The arm, too, in the shirt carries a sheen which implies he is well muscled. The face we can tell is bearded, mature but still young. The way the legs are positioned implies that, once dressed up, Judas is going to move, move away, go about business that is his own.

'From these schematic observations what do we tell? There is grandeur about this figure, a person who is engaged in an action of vast consequence. We catch him at the moment when decision turned into irrevocable action, and when he assumes his coat of black – which will make him a very dark figure indeed. Saint John says, "Judas went out. And it was night." The white background is presumably a wall with the hint of a floor. But where Judas is going is the dark, away from the place where flesh and lemon, pale blue and white, colours of life and hope, prevail. You see how from the right-hand top of the painting shadow increases: that is the direction of the future, and its presence adds to the menace of the dark that will prevail as Judas goes into action.

'You wouldn't know this was Judas if the title didn't give it away.... He represents a man trapped by his own self confidence and convictions.... There is a deep compassion in this picture of a troubled man, who is a man with our kind of trouble. This is the sort of way that Jesus might have looked on a man whom he called a friend, even though he betrayed him.'

The Empty Tomb
2008
Acrylic on canvas
121.9 x 244 cm
Collection of the Artist

5

'What Kind of Times are These?'[63]
The *365 Series*

T. S. Eliot wrote that 'human kind cannot bear very much reality'; whilst W. H. Auden in his poem, 'Musée des Beaux Arts', reminds us that suffering takes place whilst no one is paying any special attention and that despite everything, life goes on:

About suffering they were never wrong,
The Old Masters: how well they understood
Its human position: how it takes place
While someone else is eating or opening a window or just walking dully along . . .[64]

I was in London on 7 July 2005 and like so many others I was caught up in the chaos and anxiety of that day. When I returned to my studio I felt compelled to work through the experience in paint. The painting was a failure in itself, but as a cathartic act it was a success. It has not survived. A year later, I read once again about that day in my daily newspaper and was struck once more by the photographs showing the familiar streets of London transformed into a backdrop to horror. I took one of those photographs and made a small painting from it. Without realising it, I had begun what would become a daily practice. Each day I choose one image (usually from The Guardian newspaper) that strikes a particular chord with me and make a small painting from it. Each panel is 6 x 8 inches. I try to paint them as simply and as lovingly as I can. They have become a kind of vigil – a way of giving time back to the images we see every day and the individuals represented in them. Feeling powerless in the face of world events, this is one

thing I can do. When I started making the series I intended to continue each day for a year – now I see no reason to stop.

Selections from the series have been shown at different venues, including York Minster, various educational institutions and Manchester Art Gallery, but they were first seen publicly at Imperial War Museum North (IWM North). This museum was set up specifically to tell the story of how war has affected the lives of British and Commonwealth citizens since 1914, and as so much of what we know about warfare and its effect on humanity now comes into our homes via newspapers, the computer or telephone screen, images from these sources are highly charged with significance.

Although the subjects of these works mostly reflect the preponderance of images of warfare, crime and suffering that we find on a daily basis in the news media, many do not. The choosing of the images is intuitive: not every one relates to scenes of tragedy, one might be a response to a moment of anguish on the football pitch, another to the joy of a young boy jumping over a puddle. Each is dated on the reverse, but other than that, no further reference is made to the wider context of which they are a part.

This was personal activity for Ghislaine – not seen as part of her professional practice at all until a visit to the studio by the curator Michael Simpson, who initiated the exhibition at IWM North, and so what was in essence a private act has become a very public one. Its effectiveness is that they are so simple. They are painted directly from

365 Series
Ghislaine preparing for her
exhibition at Imperial War
Museum North
2009

a single photographic source and they are often experienced grouped together as a single unit. For, like Goya's series of etchings and aquatints, the *Disasters of War*, it is the cumulative effect of seeing a number of these works that gives them their authority, as much as the nature of their imagery. As each image references happenings in the real world, so the original source of some of the panels might be remembered, half-remembered by the viewer, whilst others will be encountered for the first time. Each single painting speaks to its neighbour either through shared content or perhaps through a repeated colour or shape. However it happens, connections are made and the viewer is engaged. As Degas once said, 'A painting requires a little mystery, some vagueness, and some fantasy. When you always make your meaning perfectly plain you end up boring people.'[66]

The panels, like the photographs from which they originate, include a measure of ambiguity and uncertainty and so they resonate with our lived position within the world, as we can never fully know anything and things themselves are not fixed, but exist in a constant state of flux. These ideas are a necessary part of painting or drawing and should not be understood as a shortcoming or a problem, but as a sign for the inexhaustible nature of our interaction with the world.

So many of these images are reminiscent of poses and compositions by the Old Masters, and so many of them suggest latter-day Pietàs, scenes of martyrdom or occasions of grace. This should be no surprise, for just

as photographers have learnt from painters so painters have learnt from photographers. Both groups operate as witnesses, interpreters of world events however small or significant or of whatever nature. Both share the challenge of not aestheticising horror; aware of the dangers of creating something merely beautiful, rather than something that operates as a meaningful response to the world.

Hence the significance of the words of those who have suffered and have tried to put into words something of that experience. The writer and holocaust survivor, Primo Levi, wrote that, 'The story of Auschwitz has been written almost exclusively by people who, like me, did not plumb the depths. . . . Those who were "saved" in the camps were not the best of us, rather they were the worst: the egotists, the violent, the insensitive, the collaborators .... The best all died.'[67]

Humbling words, troubling, but not disabling. Despite everything, the compulsion to respond to life in all its aspects is part of who and what we are. Modern technology brings us instant access to a constant flow of images and news items and thus, we become inescapably implicated in world events. We are all of us witnesses, but that very technology that makes us so, can also make us less responsive than perhaps we should be as we drown under a ceaseless show of information. And of course, we can always turn away or turn off. In its old-fashioned way, we believe that painting retains a specialness precisely because it is handcrafted. Also, Ghislaine's panels can be, and often are, handled, and from this simple

'Ghislaine's small paintings are like small, insistent echoes of pain. Many of the images that are presented as part of the daily news cycle are seen briefly by us – sometimes processed but seldom dwelt on. The simple act by Ghislaine of taking the time every day to respond in paint to a selected image is first and foremost an act of respect to the men, women and children caught up in the news. Tellingly, all of the images she selects to paint have a human dimension – mothers, fathers, sisters, brothers, infants – but even when the human figure is absent, such as in an image of a discarded sandal, flesh tones still dominate. We are reminded that although these are important stories, to be discussed and analysed, they all reflect lives that have often been lost, damaged or at the very least thrown off course in some way.

'Eventually, tragedy and conflict catches up with all of us, one way or another. Ghislaine herself was in London on 7/7 with all its confusion and anxieties. She could come home that evening, but others didn't, and her 365 paintings are small but heartfelt reminders that every night, someone somewhere doesn't go home.'

Michael Simpson, Head of Visual Art & Engagement, The Lowry, who instigated Ghislaine's exhibition of 365 of these works at Imperial War Museum North

action opportunity for thought is given and from reflection, action might follow.

Ghislaine's relationship with these works and her continuing practice of making them each day is a complex one, for to be painting such images in the comfort and security of the studio may seem an indulgent, voyeuristic or even futile activity, compromised at various levels, but to stop would not seem right.

On occasion she has shown a number of the *365 Series* together with selections from her suite of transcriptions of Goya's *Disasters of War* – and they fit in exactly. Goya's wide-eyed response to the Napoleonic invasion of Spain in 1808, was produced between 1810–1820 and nothing has changed since – nada.[65] The atrocities in the pictures are precise and terrifying indictements of our inability to rise out from the

moral darkness. Goya – surely the first really modern artist – shows us a world of ambiguity and is the creator of some of the most unforgettable images of human degradation and folly – images in which the horror of the subject matter is somehow reinforced by the beauty and virtuosity of his technique.

As in Goya's incomparable etchings and paintings, images can only operate at one or two, or even more removes from the reality of what they purport to represent or depict. To paraphrase Gertrude Stein, a painting is a painting is a painting. Removed from their original source and supporting texts, Ghislaine's paintings known as the *365 Series* might lead us to consider the sobering fact that knowledge is one thing – understanding another.

From the 365 Series
Oil on board
15.25 x 20.3 cm
Collection of the Artist

A selection from the 365 Series

From the 365 Series
Oil on board
20.3 x 15.25 cm
Actual Size
Collect Art

From the 365 Series
Oil on board
20.3 x 15.25 cm
Actual Size
Collect Art

A selection from the 365 Series

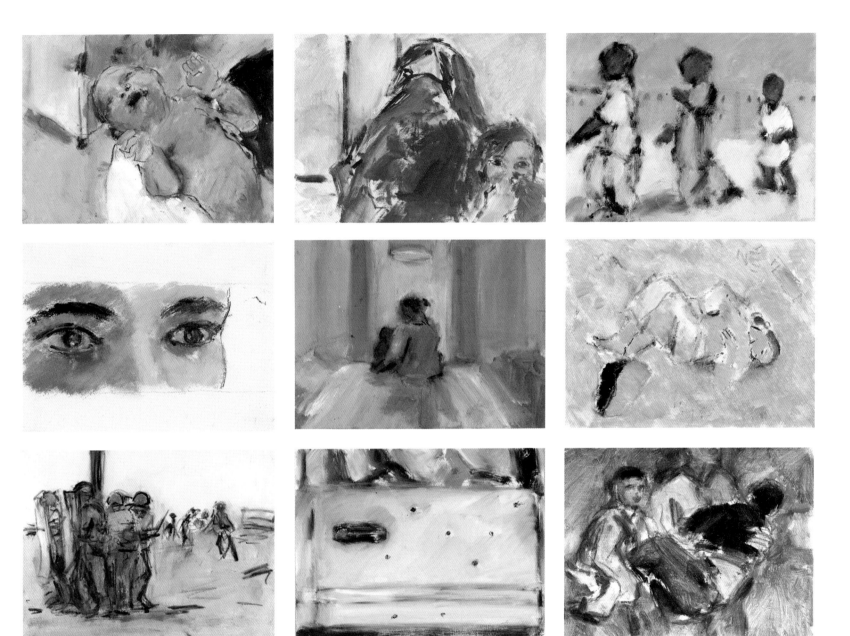

From the 365 Series
Oil on panel
20.3 x 25.4,
Private Collection

From the 365 Series
(opposite)
Acrylic on board
20.3 x 15.25 cm
Collect Art

Guantánamo Bay: the Cage
(overleaf)
2012
Acrylic on canvas
152.4 x 182.9 cm
Collection of the Artist

6

Family Life
The ground on which we stand

Max Climbing Stairs
1986
Oil on canvas
78.8 x 61 cm
Collection of the Artist

Max Watching Television
1993
Felt pen on Ingres paper
33 x 25.4 cm
Collection of the Artist

Cordelia Drawing
1990
Oil on tile
20.3 x 15.25 cm
Collection of the Artist

'Her mother and child studies have a quieter beauty expressing the protectiveness integral to this age-old symbol.'

Sister Wendy Beckett, Women Critics Select Women Artists, The Bruton Street Gallery, 1992.

It's part of painters' lore that 'if you can't find inspiration 15 feet away from where you stand, then you're not a real painter.' There is a certain amount of truth in this statement. Ghislaine's house, garden and immediate surroundings provide much inspiration for her work; for example, our kitchen window looks out over Glossop's marketplace and this real-life stage set has inspired many of Ghislaine's studies of figures in action. Our first Christmas in the house was made unforgettable by witnessing an altercation involving two drunken revellers and a frozen turkey. That particular scene never made it onto canvas, but many others have.

With few significant exceptions, the people who populate Ghislaine's canvases are painted from direct observation, filtered through numerous and often rapidly produced drawings or photographs. The latter are often taken with scant regard for technical perfection – in fact, it is normally the case that the imprecisions of a hastily taken snapshot will prove to be more suggestive than any razor-sharp image full of unnecessary detail. As long as the essentials of what has attracted her to that action have been caught, in however minimal a fashion, then all is well and good, and occasionally one will serve as a point of departure for a new work. For looking is not a simple mechanical receiving of sensory data, but rather a dynamic interaction between the observer and that which is observed. It is this interaction that a drawing or painting can capture – the mind at work as the artist tries to recreate that engagement with as much vividness as she can. These rapid-response drawings seek to suggest the *éclat* of sensory experience as economically as possible. There is little time for hesitation, for to catch life on the wing requires hard, precise looking and a responsive hand, quickened by years of practice. This allows instinct to take control so that the drawing seems to draw itself. Ghislaine is attracted to what she calls 'the unguarded moment' when people's self-

awareness is at its least evident. It may be the unselfconscious movements of a figure walking across the marketplace, or it could be someone sleeping on a train or lost in reverie at a neighbouring café table. In all of Ghislaine's work there is a marked tendency to bring the subject up close to the canvas surface; background detail, such as it is, is woven into the foreground.

This can be seen most clearly in one of Ghislaine's most recognisable subjects: the embrace, when two separate beings hold each other, an action that signifies both an offering and an acceptance. Many artists have mentioned the correlation or the kinship between oil paint and the sensual warmth and plenitude of human skin; somehow oil paint can stand as a convincing equivalent for the touch of flesh and the sharing of emotions. Ghislaine enjoys painting moments of touch, the embrace, whether rough, passionate or gentle, solicitous or protecting – each one so different, so telling – the precise, concentrated gestures that lead us back to a more conscious awareness of who and what we are. People embrace when words are not enough; language becomes secondary or even redundant and the body is trusted to do the comforting – to do the right thing.

Ghislaine's sketches and her intimate records of her daily life have become a visual diary and a reservoir of possible subjects for future paintings. Most will remain unseen in her sketchbooks but some, even the slightest

of sketches, may fire her memory, bringing back a singular moment or an interesting coincidence of forms or colours that will suggest further development. The possibilities are endless and consequently her paintings of such subjects are many and varied. They include major paintings, but often they become the subjects for small intensely worked pieces, that seek to capture the mood and atmosphere of a moment in time, be it the rapt concentration of Cordelia drawing, Max writing or myself at work at my desk. One of Ghislaine's keynote paintings, *Mother and Daughter* of 1997, was developed from such a moment. Ghislaine made a quick ballpoint sketch of herself and Cordelia standing naked, reflected in the bedroom mirror. The resulting painting expresses a shared unspoken realisation that the uninhibited freedom of childhood would soon be a thing of the past. A similar, but completely different, moment happened with Max, though in this case he was totally unaware of the significance of his actions. Ghislaine, coming downstairs, caught sight of him ironing his shirt to go out and suddenly saw him no longer as a boy, but a young man.

Self-Portrait with Max and Cordelia
(overleaf)
1987
Oil on canvas
61 x 101.6 cm
Collection of the Artist

Mother and Child (Pink)
2016
Oil on panel
30.5 x 22.8 cm
Collect Art

**Michael with Max
Contre-jour**
(above) 1984
Oil on linen
78.8 x 58.5 cm
Collection of the Artist

Michael with Cordelia
(bottom left)
1987
Oil on flax
57 x 61 cm
Collect Art

Max Dressing
1999
Oil on flax
101.6 x 61cm
Collection of the Artist

Michael Drawing with Max
1987
Oil on canvas
35.8 x 45.7 cm
Collection of the Artist

Paddling Pool Study (I)
1987
Oil on flax
45.7 x 40.7 cm
Collection of the Artist

Paddling Pool Study (II)
1987,
Oil on flax
45.7 x 40.7 cm
Collection of the Artist

Paddling Pool Study (III)
1987
Oil on flax
45.7 x 40.7 cm
Collection of the Artist

Chris with Jessie
1985
Oil on flax
127 x 101.6cm
Collection of the Artist

**Cordelia and Jessie
in the Paddling Pool**
1990
Acrylic on board
22.8 x 30.5cm
Collection of the Artist

**Max and Cordelia
in the Green Kitchen**
(opposite)
1990
Acrylic on canvas
50.8 x 40.7cm
Collection of the Artist

Max Drawing
1990
Oil on tile
15.25 x 20.3 cm
Collection of the Artist

**Evening Interior
Cordelia in Yellow**
1996
Acrylic on tile
15.25 x 15.25 cm
Collect Art

Cordelia with Flowers
1996
Acrylic on board
15.25 x 15.25 cm
Collect Art

**Cordelia Playing the
Mandolin**
1997
Oil on board
15.25 x 15.25 cm
Collect Art

**Cordelia in the Green
Kitchen**
1995
Oil on canvas
91.4 x 91.4 cm
Collection of the Artist

Flamenco Dress
(opposite)
2002
Acrylic on board
114.4 x 76.2 cm
Collection of the Artist

Cordelia Brushing her Teeth
1993
Acrylic on board
91.4 x 61 cm
Collection of the Artist

Cordelia at the Easel
1996
Oil on board
72.4 x 54.6 cm
Collection of the Artist

Cordelia Arranging her Hair
2016
Oil on flax
127 x 101.6 cm
Collect Art

Cordelia in the Studio (I)
2003
Acrylic on board
121.9 x 91.4 cm
Collection of the Artist

Cordelia in the Studio (II)
2003
Acrylic on canvas
91.4 x 61cm
Collect Art

Max on the Beach (I)
1992
Oil on board
20.3 x 15.25 cm
Collect Art

Max on the Beach (II)
1992
Oil on board
20.3 x 15.25 cm
Collection of the Artist

Max Ironing
2001
Acrylic on canvas
117 x 76.2 cm
Collection of the Artist

Cordelia by the Window
(above)
2016
Oil on board
15.25 x 20.3 cm
Collect Art

**Head of Cordelia
in Red and Black**
2016
Oil on canvas
50.8 x 40.7 cm
Collect Art

Cordelia in the Armchair
2016
Oil on board
15.25 x 20.3 cm
Collect Art

Cordelia in a Striped Dress
2016
Acrylic on panel
61 x 61cm
Collect Art

Cordelia on the Sofa
1991
Pastel on paper
22.9 x 30.5 cm
Collection of the Artist

Bedroom Chair
2007
Oil on board
61 x 61cm
Collection of the Artist

Jane in a White Dress
1988
Oil on board
45.7 x 40.7 cm
Courtesy of Gateway Gallery

My Mother: the Empty Room
(right)
2008
Acrylic on board
96.5 x 61 cm
Collection of the Artist

THE FUNERAL PAINTING

At the other end of the spectrum from the fullness of life is the stillness of death and its aftermath. As Ghislaine painted a memorable large canvas entitled *Max: the First Day* in 1984, so in 1993 she painted *The Corridor*, or as we call it, the 'Death Bed' painting, inspired by a small indistinct black-and-white newspaper photograph. Both paintings find an echo in the weighty *Empty Tomb* painting of 2000 and a number of works that she painted of her father during his final illness. But for us, one of the most poignant of Ghislaine's paintings is *Flowers for My Father*, in which three generations of women stand by her father's graveside in Birr, County Offaly, his widow, granddaughter and daughter. As Shakespeare never tired of telling us, art can keep memories alive, it can grant to us transient beings a certain spurious immortality. Although a painter can no more stop time than anyone else, yet there are certain paintings that almost seem to defy this brutal fact. Ghislaine's painting of herself, her mother and our daughter preserves a memory of that moment, rather than the moment itself, that is lost to time as surely as her father. And so it operates as a kind of a talisman that marks in all its complex layering, something of the effects of loss, respect, love and togetherness without slipping into sentimentality.

Flowers for My Father
2004
152.4 x 121.9 cm
Acrylic on canvas
Collection of the Artist

7

The Unguarded Moment
Eros – for life

Couple on a Divan
2007
Monotype
17.8 x 12.7 cm
Collection of the Artist

The Red Canopy
(opposite)
2007
Oil on cardboard
36.8 x 26.7 cm
Collection of the Artist

There is magic in unfamiliar surroundings that you know will soon become familiar. Hotel rooms have this particular quality, and a strange city becomes less alien once you have settled into your room. The anonymity of the decor of most hotel rooms only enhances the sensation of living in a room that has seen so much, a place that is at once open to all, but now, for a short period, is your own private space. Ghislaine delights in such ideas and finds inspiration in the unexpected scenarios that result from carrying out the mundane actions of everyday life in unfamiliar settings, in which taking a shower, brushing her hair or catching herself in the mirror are given an extra resonance by the novelty of the situation.

The transitory nature of one's stay in such places can be convincingly evoked in the loose handling of paint, the washed-out colours and the tremulous drawing that defines but also obscures the room's details to give an aura of mystery and expectation. Something that might be small and insignificant in itself, yet when seen in unfamiliar surroundings, will open up and reveal itself in a very different perspective. For example, an expanse of wallpaper split by a slant of falling light, or the soft incandescence of a bedside lamp that bathes the room in a muted glow or casts unexpected shadows, such small happenings can trigger entire compositions. Doors and windows, balconies and mirrors; all become potential for unfolding pictorial dramas. No wonder then, that such artists as Van Eyck, Vermeer, Monet, were all attracted to the compositional possibilities that mirrors offer. Ghislaine is no different: they are all intrigued by those silvered surfaces, such perfect analogies for the play of interior and exterior spaces, the within and without – whether of the body or the mind. As we observe these interiors, we find ourselves party to a disconcerting turn of events.

Does the image look out or do we look in? Are we meant to really be there or are we invisible? To add a painted mirror to this scenario only adds to the confusion. If we believe in the painted mirror, even for a moment, then why do we not find ourselves reflected in it?

Sometimes the intimacy of a hotel bedroom can make one sensitive to unexpected aspects of paintings that one thought one knew well. Coming back to the hotel after a long time spent in front of Velasquez's *Las Meninas*, Ghislaine noticed a correlation between the edge of the bedspread reflected in the hotel room mirror and the flowing rhythms of the edge of the dresses in that great painting – a relationship compounded by seeing me in the background, with my arm raised to draw the curtains – and a few months later, Ghislaine began an entire series of paintings dedicated to the possibilities inherent in that very subject – the *Madrid Suite*, based on drawings she had made in the hotel room.

Although many artists have drawn or sketched small works relating to their private lives or the erotic, it is relatively unusual for artists to paint, as Ghislaine does, large celebratory canvases of such intimate moments. The subject is more associated with the private and immediate process of drawing – it is a real challenge for an artist to keep those qualities in more finished works. We prize such images as records of a shared love that preserve moments of intimacy. Ghislaine's engagement with such subjects is partly a reaction against the prurience and restrictive nature of a Catholic upbringing. Her images of lovemaking for example, are neither gratuitous nor prurient, but simply part of our lives, to be remembered, celebrated, shared and relived though the picture-making process. Imbued with an unsentimental intimacy, they are suggestive of a poignant understanding of time passing and a deep respect for the importance of the physical touch. Ghislaine leaves out all unnecessary details, concentrating only on the essential elements necessary for conveying the thrill of it all. For the artist, painting is not just about producing a finished object; they are also acts of *jouissance:* the sheer pleasure of

painting. Painting can be an indulgence in the passionate delight of pigment, colour, spontaneous action and the acts of remembrance and creation. The making is the artist's privilege, whilst looking is the viewer's – and there is a difference between the two positions.

Ghislaine's agitated brushwork and impetuous improvisatory technique allows her to find a convincing equivalent to match the tumultuous and passionate aspects of this subject.

As mentioned above, the erotic work of many artists is found mostly in their private drawings, a medium that corresponds well to these intimate aspects of our lives. However, it is a subject that is particularly well-suited to monotype, a strange hybrid technique that exists in the hinterland somewhere between drawing and painting. Monotype is a term that covers a multitude of different processes in which the image is worked directly into an ink-covered surface. One of Ghislaine's preferred ways of working is to lay a sheet of paper over an inked glass plate. She then draws onto the paper which, when lifted from the glass, retains an inked image on its underside – the subtleties of the medium are the result of the varying pressure of the pencil point, palm of her hand or fingers that give her monotypes their particular quality. It is a fluid medium and as the image is fugitive, only one good image can be made. It has very special characteristics as it can be left as it is or enriched with an overlay of pastel.

Woman on a Balcony
2016
Oil on panel
61 x 91.4 cm
Courtesy of Art Decor Gallery

Hotel Room, Malaga
(overleaf)
2016
Oil on panel
61 x 121.9 cm
Collection of the Artist

Lovers
2002
Oil on canvas
127 x 76.2 cm
Collection of the Artist

Naked Embrace
2002
Oil on canvas
153.4 x 101.6 cm
Collection of the Artist

ghislaine Howards 2011   A/P

An Intimate Embrace
1997
Oil on canvas
121.9 x 76.2 cm
Collection of the Artist

An Intimate Embrace
2011
Drypoint
17.8 x 14 cm
Collection of the Artist

Passions
(above)
2016
Graphite and acrylic on paper
30.5 x 40.7 cm
Collection of the Artist

Passionate Embrace
2011
Drypoint
17.8 x 12.7 cm
Collection of the Artist

**Naked Self-Portrait
Hotel Room**
2011
Drypoint
17.8 x 12.7 cm
Collection of the Artist

Ghislaine Howard 2011   A/P.

Intimate Scene
(overleaf)
2010
Oil on canvas
61 x 91.4 cm
Collect Art

The Unguarded Moment   **186**

Michael Reclining
2014
Graphite and watercolour on
paper
22.8 x 15.25 cm
Collection of the Artist

**Drawing from the Mirror
Madrid**
2006
Acrylic and pigment on board
122.x 61 cm
Collection of the Artist

Michael Dressing
2016
Oil on board
91.4 x 61 cm
Collection of the Artist

Woman at the Mirror
2015
Oil on board
30.5 x 22.8 cm
Collect Art

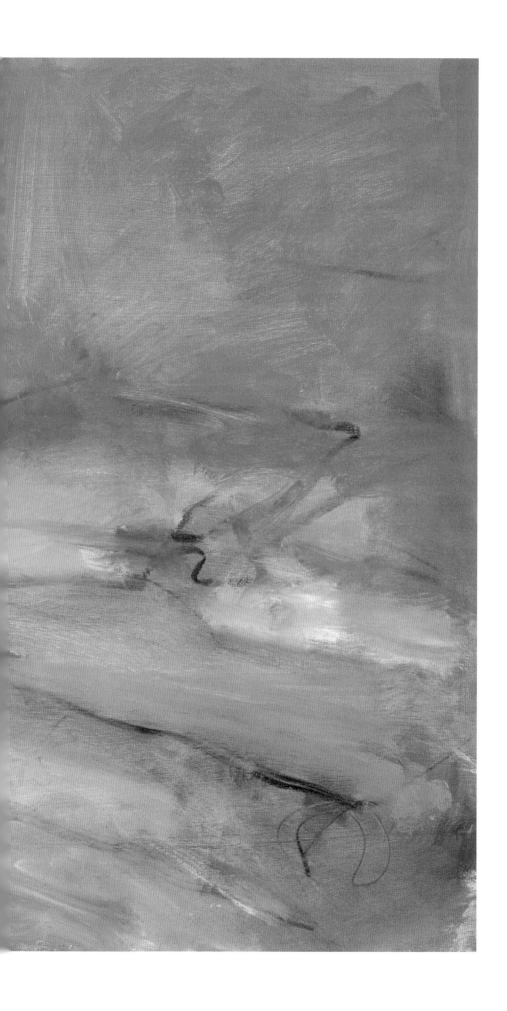

Making the Bed
2016
Oil on panel
61 x 91.4 cm
Collect Art

Hotel Room, Melbourne
2016
Oil on panel
61 x 121.9 cm
Collection of the Artist

8

Self-Portraits
Through a glass darkly

Ghislaine has painted self-portraits at irregular intervals throughout her life. When viewed together, they present a compelling catalogue of time and circumstance at work. The viewer can see her face and body over four decades, responding to the physical facts of what it is to be human. Like geographical terrain, the face bears signs on its outward form of the forces that remain hidden beneath. To paint one's own portrait is a paradoxical procedure, for we know ourselves better than anyone and yet we hardly know ourselves at all. Self-portraiture goes right to the heart of what it is to make sense of the visual. As we look at the world, what we actually see is a weave of colour and tones that, by drawing or painting, we bring into order. In attempting this we set into action a dynamic between the real, what is 'out there' and the means used to represent it. This dynamic gives the painting its particular character: its 'expressiveness'. The struggle to express the real hits home hardest when an artist attempts a self-portrait. One can paint from a photograph or a drawing, but the most obdurate challenge of all perhaps, is to paint directly from a mirror reflection.

As mentioned earlier, a mirror presents us with an impenetrable conundrum – who am I? The reflection we see results from our presence before the mirror, but for all its immediacy, we can never see or know ourselves entirely. We remain distant from ourselves. However closely we peer, there is always that nagging thought – is that really me? The story of Narcissus lies at the heart of such matters and though the painted image is only an echo of the mirror, it carries a bitter truth in its shallow surface. In

more ways than one, it is a place for self-reflection. In Jean Cocteau's 1960 film, *The Testament of Orpheus (Le Testament d'Orphée)*, Heurtebise, Death's chauffeur says, 'I give you the secret of secrets. Mirrors are gates through which the dead come and go. All of you, look at your life in a mirror and you see Death at work.' The self-distancing that a mirror gives, allows the artist the opportunity to position themselves, spatially and psychologically, into the world – and its mysteries. Anyone who looks at their own reflection in a mirror knows that this process cannot but include some form of analysis of the visible and hidden self.

These are only a few of the reasons why artists find the phenomenon of the self-portrait so fascinating. There are many others: as a technical exercise, or as a means to image themselves at work, or perhaps as a form of professional aggrandisement or reassurance by setting oneself within the long tradition of other self-portraits. On a practical level, the self may be the most understanding model an artist can find. But the artist can never be complacent for, as her restless gaze traces the public image suggested by the outward phenomenon she sees before her in the mirror, her every brush mark only serves to highlight the inaccessibility of the private self that rests hidden beneath the skin's surface.

To watch this doppelgänger take form before one's eyes, patched together with touches of line and dabs and dashes of colour, is disconcerting. Each mark can only reference a moment that has just passed, never the present

Self-Portrait with a Hand Mirror
1998
Oil on panel
127 x 101.6 cm
Collection of the Artist

Self-Portrait with a Camera
2007
Acrylic on canvas
40.7 x 50.8 cm
Collect Art

The Pink and Black Dress
1997
Acrylic on canvas
182.9 x 91.4 cm
Collection of the Artist

Self-Portrait: Bedroom Mirror
2013
Acrylic on canvas
127 x 101.6 cm
Collection of the Artist

Self-Portrait with Hand Mirror, Back View
2013
Acrylic on panel
91.4 x 61 cm
Collection of the Artist

**Pregnant Self-Portrait with
Yellow Beads**
1987
Oil on canvas
50.8 x 40.7 cm
Collection of the Artist

**Pregnant Self-Portrait in
Pink**
1984
Oil on board
53.3 x 40.7 cm
Collect Art

**Pregnant Self-Portrait:
Leaning**
1987
Oil on flax
45.7 x 61 cm
Collection of the Artist

Pregnant Self-Portrait Standing
1984
Oil on canvas
76.2 x 55.9 cm
Collection of the Artist

Pregnant Self-Portrait with a Gold Necklace
1987
Oil on panel
71.1 x 55.9 cm
Collection of the Artist

Pregnant Self-Portrait with Raised Arm
1987
Charcoal on paper
76.2 x 55.9 cm
Collection of the Artist

moment. In this manner, the ultimate futility of painting reveals itself. Painting can only ever capture lost time. As the eye moves to the paper away from the self seen in the mirror, each mark can only be a trace of that brief encounter set down on canvas, and the painting or the drawing itself, only an accumulation of such traces – hence perhaps, the melancholy aspect of so many self-portraits.

This would seem to be the case in many of Ghislaine's images of herself. They can possess a sort of desperateness as traces of the brush are caught in the paint surface as if to proclaim, 'I am here' only to realise that perhaps it should say 'I was here.' They are veritable battlegrounds as she struggles with herself and her craft. They are often painted in a direct and vigorous style, wet-on-wet, areas of paint in constant interaction with each and marked by swift but effective brushwork. The painting alters, changes mood as it is worked on (as does Ghislaine too, of course) and there is a constant wiping out and repainting, shifting the pose but leaving traces of those decisions, as if to give a sense of movement and vitality. Other portraits are more tentative, as if acknowledging the impossibility or immensity of the task in hand. There is never a transparency of meaning in art and never a 'true portrait' or 'likeness', and that is the very fascination of the business. We lift one mask, only to find another. In *The Picture of Dorian Gray*, first published in 1890, Oscar Wilde wrote: 'Every portrait that is painted with feeling is a portrait of the artist, not of the sitter. The sitter is merely the accident, the occasion. It is not he who

is revealed by the painter, it is rather the painter, who on the coloured canvas, reveals himself.'

Such ideas have a long history in western art. There is a famous Tuscan saying of the medieval period, 'Ogni pittore dipinge sé' (Every painter paints himself), a statement familiar to artists as various as Leonardo, Poussin, Picasso and Hockney.

Although for many artists self-portraits can be exercises – test beds for painterly techniques – with Romanticism the self-portrait became a site of special concern, as a place to investigate the changing nature of the artist's own self. A specifically modern idea and a seductive one, but one to be treated with caution. Some of Ghislaine's most haunting, angst-ridden self-portraits are actually the result of time passing and the effort involved in trying to trap her ever-changing face reflected in the mirror onto the canvas. In other words, trying the impossible. It is a curious fact that some of her later portraits give an appearance of a younger Ghislaine, whilst some of the earlier ones make her look much older, even haggard. The impossibility of ever finding the true self-image is beautifully expressed in the following lines:

From mirror after mirror,
No vanity's displayed:
I'm looking for the face I had
Before the world was made.[68]

Self-Portrait
1999
Oil on canvas
53.3 x 43.2 cm
Collection of the Artist

9

To Pit Oneself Against Excellence[69]
'Aun aprendo' ('Still learning')

Study from Las Meninas
1998
Watercolour on lining paper
29.2 x 22.8 cm
Collection of the Artist

But I cannot deny my past to which my self is wed,
The woven figure cannot undo its thread.
'Valediction'
Louis MacNeice

Both Ghislaine and I share a deep fascination with the history of art; it is the core of my professional practice and for her, a source of inexhaustible inspiration, reassurance and challenge. In her student works we can see her directly addressing those artists she admired, freely paraphrasing their images and in the process possessing them and re-forming them into her own ambitious, but troubled work.

All art is hard work, and hard won. In copying ready-made images, artists are simply continuing a practice familiar to us all from childhood: the co-ordinating of hand and eye, and body and imagination to gain mastery of the mechanics of the visual. Like all artists, Ghislaine learns primarily from her own experience, but also from the example of others who have gone before. As painters as various as Delacroix, Degas, Picasso, Pollock and Auerbach have made evident, one is never too old to learn. The young Michelangelo, for example, copied paintings by Giotto in the church of Santa Croce in Florence, and artists such as Picasso and Frank Auerbach have continued that youthful practice as a lifelong need.

It was a central tenet of Rembrandt's teaching – he made his students copy his own drawings line for line – however, such exercises soon take on a life of their own, and become a source of deep communion. There is also a more prosaic aspect to copying – it is a useful way of breaking into the working day, a way of warming up, of getting into the zone that will allow further artistic activity to follow. And, for Dufy at least, it was as he said, a necessary way to relieve the 'itch in the fingers'. But as the itch is assuaged, and the drawing gets underway, so the eye and mind begin to seek out not some pedantic imitation of the original, but a more challenging interaction – to seek out the indefinable qualities that draw one to certain models. These models are often works of art where it is evident that something has been solved and the challenge (and deep pleasure) for the artist is to use the simplest means to try to uncover how and why this has been achieved.

Interpretation is a more exact word than copying, for the artist sitting before her chosen work becomes like a pianist sitting before a piece of music by Bach or Schubert. Musicians do not simply copy what is before them, the squiggles of ink on white paper, but give form to the sounds those marks represent. So, each drawing is an interpretation, giving the original work the opportunity to sing in a different key. Intense looking is informed by an equally intense intellectual and artistic engagement, fused together by the performative action of re-creation. As the drawing gets underway so an intimate dialogue begins with the work under scrutiny and the artist feels a direct connection with its maker.

Study after Las Meninas
2015
Acrylic on canvas
50.8 x 40.7 cm
Collect Art

This living dynamic is one of the most thrilling and seductive aspects of 'copying' the masters. For every work of art, whenever or wherever it was produced, is experienced by the viewer in the here and now, in the contemporary moment. Once encountered, something of it remains in our memories: latent perhaps, but always ready to emerge to inspire and direct our actions. This is even more the case for artists, as Picasso affirmed: 'To me there is no past or future in art. If a work of art cannot live always in the present, it must not be considered at all. The art of the Greeks, of the Egyptians, of the great painters who lived in other times is not an art of the past, perhaps it is more alive today than it ever was.'[70]

Copying another's work is a way of finding a harmonious and powerful fusion between past and present, between the work of a 'master' and one's own struggling self, and to work between the past and the present, negotiating differing ideologies, styles and subject matter.

Connecting with such works calls for a complete absorption in the search for, and expression of, the essential features of the work in question, and in the process the artist becomes once more a student. For Ghislaine never merely copies indiscriminately. Instead she selects her objects of study carefully and considers the drawing as a way of ensuring her gaze is slow and critical, a tool for investigation, reflection and invention, teasing out the potential solutions to the perennial problems that confront any serious painter.

Study after Titian's Sacred and Profane Love (c.1514)
2014
Ink on paper
25.4 x 25.4 cm
Collection of the Artist

Study after Titian's Three Ages of Man (1512–14)
2014
Ink on paper
25.4 x 25.4 cm
Collection of the Artist

Study after Titian's Annunciation (c.1562–4)
2014
Ink and watercolour on paper
20.3 x 12.7 cm
Collection of the Artist

Ghislaine does not just look at works of art; she draws from them, both literally and metaphorically. A practice shared by many artists, including Degas, who provocatively stated that, 'No art was ever less spontaneous than mine. What I do is the result of reflection and of the study of the great masters; of inspiration, spontaneity, temperament, I know nothing.'[71]

Indeed, there is nothing programmatic in Ghislaine's choices; she is driven by a need to reassert herself within the field of her practice and to find answers to her ambitions, the problems and challenges that are a fundamental aspect of her daily practice. Even if the fullness of the original work's meaning or subject matter might be outmoded or obscure, it may still offer riches to be mined: the opportunity to dig deep and find within the original material something that remains relevant for us today: its inner workings or sometimes its sheer technical accomplishment.

One crucial aspect of a copy is the speed or otherwise with which it is made. A slow calculated response allows for a considered analysis achieved over a period of time, but rapidly made studies, though less exact, can capture the immanent moment of experiencing the original work – the shock of the encounter and the richness of discovery that comes with a more intuitive, but equally concentrated, approach. Sometimes when fully absorbed in the process, one gets the illusion of direct communication with the mind and hand of the maker. As Alfredo Casella said of Debussy's piano playing, 'he made the impression of playing directly on the strings of the instrument with no intermediate mechanism – the effect was a miracle of poetry.'[72]

As in music, total immersion in the inner workings of the original can lead to the production of countless variations made over a prolonged period of time. Each return reveals something new as Ghislaine explores, excavates and rebuilds; every time taking on a particular theme or aspect of the original and running with it. The original art work may not change – but her understanding of it will, as each encounter charts yet another attempt to cut to the essentials of the work through the concentrated activity of trying to recreate it. Such discoveries are made by the process itself. The resulting transcription need not, will not, be exact, but it should capture the aura of the work, its hidden structures.

**Study after Bonnard's
The French Window
Morning at Le Cannet (1932)**
Pencil and watercolour
15.24 x 20.3 cm
Collection of the Artist

However, the presiding emotion that governs Ghislaine's practice in this area is the sheer pleasure that she feels as her eye and hand follow the forms, colours and ideas of those works that connect in some way with her own sensibilities or concerns. In fact, becoming so intimately involved with the work of another can be a sensual, even an erotic, experience as the eye reaches out and embraces both the work being copied and the one that is forming beneath the artist's hand.

Painting can be a solitary business and in studying, copying and interpreting the work of her chosen painters, Ghislaine becomes part of their company, learning from them and keeping something of what they have to offer alive. Though every conversation with another work of art is a testing ground, a battlefield, paradoxically it is also a solace, a place of reassurance. 'I have studied the art of the masters and the art of the moderns, avoiding any preconceived system and without prejudice.' These words of the nineteenth-century artist, Gustave Courbet, suggest something that I'm sure most artists feel instinctively, that we are in history and not apart from it. Linear, progressional histories are of little help to artists who prize the freedom to weave their own tapestry and who delight in the possibilities that arise with each encounter with the art of the past.

The poet Sylvia Plath declared that 'the poets I delight in are possessed by their poems as by the rhythms of their own breathing. Their finest poems seem born all of a piece, not put together by hand...'[73]

Though Plath was talking about poetry, her comments apply to all the arts. The Old Masters were highly trained and highly skilled professionals, they gained through their training a knowledge and a confidence that few contemporary artists can possess. The qualities mentioned by Plath were the result of their historical situation – one we do not share and so Ghislaine's interpretations strive to capture that lightness of being – and the struggle to do so gives a tension, even, perhaps a desperate edge to her work as she strives to wrest from their works a means of finding an equivalency in her own practice for their consummate achievements. For however slow or painstaking their genesis, the works of the great masters pulse with an inner life and remain, it seems, ever relevant. Though situated in the past, they remain dynamically alive in our present. And of course, to engage and interpret such works is to enter an apprenticeship that has no end.

Before some works, such as Velasquez's *Las Meninas*, one hesitates. It's as if what is being offered is simply too much, but as one enters the work, one breathes and inhabits that atmosphere and passes into a sort of other space where few have dared travel. An illusion, of course, but a powerful one, nevertheless. For Ghislaine, the act of drawing and painting from the masters is to accept the guiding hand they offer. They are ever generous and each encounter with a particular painting or sculpture may lead to new discoveries that might be capitalised upon, and so enrich her own resources. Sometimes this is a conscious action, perhaps the need to solve a problem, but just as often it operates at a more intuitive level. An example is her *Hotel Room, Madrid*, inspired by the compositional structure of Velasquez's great painting. Ghislaine remembers:

As I was drawing, I found myself following the slow flowing rhythms of the beautiful dresses and how they related to the dusty pink of the floor. Our hotel room was dominated by a large mirror and I was thinking of in some way using the reflection as a possible homage to the Velasquez. I sketched and took some photographs, but as I worked on the painting back home I didn't realise until the painting was well underway, how that part of the Meninas had unexpectedly found itself echoed in the fall of the bedclothes.

Such reinvention is its own reward, for though the study of the art of others is important, so is the need to preserve one's own voice. As Judy Garland advised, 'Always be a first-rate version of yourself, instead of a second-rate version of somebody else.'[74]

As Frank Auerbach said, 'Great Rembrandts shake you. There is a tension between unity and difference; one great wave or wind holding it all together as one ... I have never failed to be moved by Rembrandt.

... When I was young, I felt like I was in the ring with them. Now I just need their help. Recently Delacroix has been present, and Picasso is always there, exhorting me to be naughtier. ... painting has its own code of honour; it is our battlefield. Unless you try and do something in the shadow of these great people then it's all pointless.'[75]

Such ideas are integral to Ghislaine's work, as she tries to make an art that, though of its time, reaches beyond the specific to more universal themes and hits hard those who encounter it.

Study after Michelangelo's Dying Slave (1513–1516)
2013
Graphite on paper
18.4 x 14 cm
Collection of the Artist

L. S. Lowry
Portrait of Ann
1957
Oil on board
35.5 x 30.5cm
© The Lowry Collection, Salford

Self-Portrait with Blue Headscarf
1981
Oil on canvas
58.4 x 43.cm
Collection of the Artist

Across a span of almost 30 years the direct gaze of Lowry's 'Ann' is evoked in Ghislaine's own steady engagement with the viewer in this self-portrait painted shortly after she moved back to Eccles after several years away in Newcastle, London and France. Direct as her gaze is, her candid self-assessment is nonetheless more questioning, more self-exploratory than Ann's unknowable, impassive and challenging stare. Subtle, rich, autumnal shades contrast starkly with the red, black and white of Ann's mask-like countenance, creating a portrait no less arresting but flesh and blood, both strong and vulnerable, claiming our attention and engagement.

Claire H Stewart
Curator, The Lowry Collection

Lowry described *Coming from the Mill* as 'his most characteristic mill scene' and it has become one of his most iconic, best known paintings. *Going Home in the Snow* and *Young Man Walking* could almost be details from Lowry's larger scene – real yet anonymous individuals, slouching along with hands in pockets, or trudging with heads bent to their destinations. The horizontal line of the pavement edge running across the bottom of *Young Man Walking* is a classic Lowry device – a simple delineation of space and place which at the same time creates a small but significant distance between the viewer and the figure subject. En masse Lowry's figures create patterns of movement across his canvas while simultaneously possessing a stillness as individuals. Using an almost equally reduced palette but with looser, broader brushstrokes, Ghislaine's figures have the immediacy of one of Lowry's scribbled pencil drawings, swiftly executed on the spot, caught for a moment before hurrying on their way.

Claire H Stewart,
Curator, The Lowry Collection

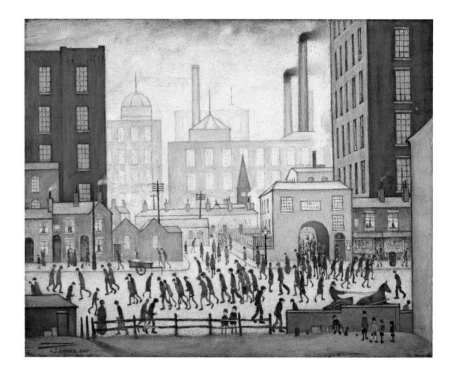

L. S. Lowry
Coming From the Mill
1930
Oil on canvas
42 x 52 cm
© The Lowry Collection
Salford

Young Man Walking
Glossop
2015
Acrylic on panel
61 x 61 cm
Collect Art

Going Home in the Snow
1982
Oil on panel
20.3 x 30.5 cm
Private Collection

Ghislaine's familiarity with the work of L. S. Lowry from childhood surfaces as a recurring thread in her painting. The study of people going about their everyday lives and unremarkable errands shares some details in common with Lowry – a child in a pram with an older sibling alongside; a dog, apparently wandering free with a mind of its own; the sense of figures moving in and out of the canvas, made static for a moment in paint. More so than in Lowry's market place, however, the people depicted at Cross Lane Market feel like individuals – real women and children, caught for an instant against the vibrant colours of the market stalls. Beyond any details of composition, what essentially links both artists is a fascination and empathy for their fellow human beings, their intimate observation of our routines and the significance of the small incidental moments that bind us together.

Claire H Stewart
Curator, The Lowry Collection

Cross Lane Market
1970
Acrylic on canvas
30.5 x 40.7 cm
Collect Art

L. S. Lowry
Market Scene Northern Town
1939
Oil on canvas
45.7 x 61.1 cm
© The Lowry Collection, Salford

Sketchbook Pages
Seven studies after Goya's
Disasters of War (1810–20)
with a drawing from a
contemporary news image
bottom right
(opposite)
2011
Pen and ink
(Each 15.25 x 20.3cm)
Collection of the Artist

**After Goya, Disparate
puntual from Los disparates
(c.1815–23)**
Acrylic and pigment on canvas
127 x 101.6 cm
Collect Art

Writing of the original painting by Goya, Jean Clair observed: '...a young woman balances on the back of a horse, which in turn appears to be balancing on a flexible cord, like a tightrope walker – an impossible feat, and one that is apparently unnoticed by the crowd in the background. Goya skilfully plays with illusion here, for the horse's hooves and the cord are, in fact, firmly on the ground. This becomes clear when one focuses on the crowd; the spectators are not positioned below the horse, looking upwards, but behind it, on the same level, looking down. Thus the horse is not a real tightrope walker after all, and this image may be a bitter comment on the general credulity of ordinary Spaniards.'

The Great Parade: Portrait of the Artist as Clown, 2004

**Study after Poussin's
A Bacchanalian Revel
Before a Term (1632–3)**
2016
Oil on linen
50.8 x 61cm
Collect Art

**Jubilation: Women's
Football Team**
2015
Oil on canvas
61 x 91.4 cm
Collect Art

Study after Poussin's
The Entombment (1559)
2013
Oil on flax
101.6 x 127 cm
Collection of the Artist

Velasquez Las Meninas
(opposite)
1656
Oil on canvas
318 x 276 cm
Prado, Madrid

**Study after Velasquez's
Las Meninas**
2015
Oil on board
91.4 x 101.6 cm
Private Collection
Photograph courtesy of Art
Decor Gallery

**After Rembrandt's
The Three Crosses**
2001
Acrylic on canvas
50.8 x 61 cm
Collection of the Artist

**Ercole di Roberti Pietà
(Predella of Stories of
Christ: 2)**
1482
Oil on wood
33 x 30 cm
Courtesy National Museums
Liverpool, Walker Art Gallery

After Ercole di Roberti's Pietà:
2007
Acrylic on panel
61 x 91.44 cm
Collection of the Artist

**Tightrope Walker
Self-Portrait**
2010
Monotype with pastel
10.2 x 15.25 cm
Collection of the Artist

10

'The Circus Animals' Desertion'
'I sought a theme...'

We cannot always live in the real world, though the world of the imagination surely is intimately connected to the world of our everyday existence. We need the imaginary and the resources it offers to play, learn, to look back and to look forward. The potency of myths and the archetypes they suggest, in whatever shape they might take, are needed.

The gods, the pagan heroes and heroines of old are not dead, merely sleeping, rousing themselves in the half-light of memory and finding themselves reborn in poems, novels and films – residing to varying degrees in our memories, changing their significance according to those who imagine and dream – they survive. The stories of their doings reverberate in our art and literature – from their earliest manifestations in ancient history to their latest manifestations in popular culture, playing out familiar themes, a part of our personal imaginative landscape. Their abiding presence cannot be ignored in the galleries and art books where the images from Ovid and Greek mythology are seen alongside images from the Christian tradition. The richness and diversity of pagan beliefs have found themselves figured, in all kinds of permutations, at every level of our cultural lives. In a review of James Joyce's *Ulysses*, written in 1923, T. S. Eliot wrote, 'It is here that Mr. Joyce's parallel use of the *Odyssey* has a great importance. ... In using the myth, in manipulating a continuous parallel between contemporaneity and antiquity, Mr. Joyce is pursuing a

method which others must pursue after him. ... Instead of the narrative method, we may now use the mythical method. It is, I seriously believe, a step toward making the modern world possible for art.'[76]

It's not really a new phenomenon at all, for many artists have followed this path over the years, each acting out their own understandings of this abiding idea. So many artists from Velasquez to Lord Leighton, Picasso to Beckmann and Bacon – not to mention any number of more recent artists – have made fruitful use of this idea each shaping the ancient stories to suit their own interests.[77] Many of Ghislaine's themes can be traced back directly or indirectly to Ovid's *Metamorphoses*, which since its composition has been a tremendous resource for artists and poets. But it is above all the images that the Old Masters and Picasso made from this text that has given her permission to treat these stories in a personal way – to invent, interpret and play with these perennial themes in manners that may be deeply serious or pleasurably playful.

These classical figures give me an excuse to play with narrative and the nude; to present a series of meetings and encounters, dramatising my own life in disguised form, partly real, partly fantastical – subverting Picasso's overtly male perspective to one that is distinctly feminine: Picasso had the Minotaur – I prefer the centauress. These works are mostly, but not always,

playful meditations, daydreams. I have always loved his work – in all its forms: his virtuosity, imagination, creative energy and erotic force. But there is another Picasso: the Picasso of slumber and rest, the watcher and the watched.

There is another great source of inspiration that has supported Ghislaine's practice. For us both, the poetry of W.B. Yeats has been a significant force in our imaginative and creative lives. Yeats can be playful or deadly serious in his thinking and use of myth and legend – he brooded long and hard on such things all his life. Amongst all his powerful poems, one above all has struck a major chord with Ghislaine: 'The Circus Animals' Desertion' that became the leitmotif in an exhibition that took place in Ireland in 2010.[78] The exhibition included work that was highly personal and emotive in nature as Ghislaine reflected upon that great poem and set its words into her own life, her childhood dreams and adult ambitions. The suite of images that followed pictured not only the dark days (and nights) of the soul, but also the mysterious energising power of the imagination. Such ideas correspond with Francis Bacon's 1962 statement: 'What is fascinating now is that it's going to become more difficult for the artist, because he must really deepen the game to be any good at all.'[78] And as ever, the 'he' in such statements stung her into a renewed sense of her own feminine self. In the following essay, the noted Irish art historian and writer Fionna Barber, Reader in Art History at Manchester School of Art, discusses some of the ideas suggested by Ghislaine's engagement with the poetry of W. B. Yeats.

'After They've Gone':
W. B. Yeats 'The Circus Animals' Desertion', Gender, Creativity and Irishness in the Work of Ghislaine Howard

It begins with a sofa, a woman's body lying across its worn cushions. This is a theme familiar from the grand tradition of European painting, enabling artists to display both their skill in representing the nude female model, while also playing to the eroticised gaze of the male viewer. Yet already we are in a place where tradition is both invoked and changed; this is Ghislaine Howard's studio and the couch is actually a much-loved family relic. It is also her own body, curled up away from our eyes, a sleeper protecting the dreams she nurtures.

These monotypes, drawings and paintings are part of a wider group of loosely linked works that marked the eventual resolution of a period of uncertainty and doubt, both suggesting new directions and affirming deeper themes within the artist's work. For Ghislaine these issues were crystallised by a re-reading of W. B. Yeats's poem 'The Circus Animals'

Desertion' (1938), written towards the end of his life, at a time of great personal uncertainty. Unable to tap into the deep mythological themes that fed the inner poetic vision of his work, by the late 1930s the role of these themes – and indeed that of his own poetry and plays – in a fiery engendering of a new Irish nation was becoming exhausted. Indeed, for Yeats, who had taken to wintering in the South of France for the last years of his life, Ireland and Irishness were now seen through the double lens of distance and memory, while all around him dark atavistic forces were pushing Europe towards further catastrophe. The paired circus animals – mythology and nation – had slipped the poet's traces and now caused havoc in the world at large.

A constant concern in Ghislaine's work for some years now (the *365 Series*) has been the role of painting as an act of acknowledgement of the small acts of mercy and kindness that take place in conditions of great political turmoil in the contemporary world – conditions in many ways not dissimilar to those when Yeats was writing his last poems. However, my concern here is to draw attention to some other aspects of the significance of Yeats's poem – and Yeats as a poet – in relation to some of her work at this time.

These are focused on two main themes: firstly, Ghislaine's role as a woman painter who has always claimed her position in relation to the grand tradition of European culture, of which Yeats forms a part, but from which women have historically been excluded as artists or poets.

Yellow Studio
The Artist at Work
2014
Acrylic on board
61 x 91.4 cm
Collection of the Artist

I must lie down where all ladders start ... GA. 2010.

Yet Ghislaine has always recognised the significance of her identity as a woman artist in relation to this canonical history. A further significant outcome of this period of doubt and uncertainty for example, has been a dialogue with the work of Picasso, focused around the role of the artist in her studio. Secondly, as a painter from a family where Irishness was important; although Ghislaine was born in Eccles in Greater Manchester, her mother, Maureen, is originally from County Carlow and spent much of her early life in Birr, County Offaly. The family have always maintained strong connections to Ireland. And as is so often the case for the daughters and sons of Irish parents who live elsewhere, this also takes the form of a psychological linking of places. For Ghislaine, a ruined distillery in Birr bought by her parents in 1992 has become imaginatively associated with Yeats's home in nearby Galway, the Thoor Ballylee, its rural setting and accompanying memories an important source of inspiration. The cultural realm of Yeats's poetry and the life of the artist's family thus become fused in an inner world of experience.

So much of Ghislaine's extensive body of work, however, is rooted in the observable world – the acute perception of human behaviour, the compassionate depiction of movement and gesture, or the nurturing relationships between mothers (and fathers) and their children. But what happens when that vision falters, when a previously clear path becomes indistinct? Eventually, the realisation grows that uncertainty is the only condition from which one can move forward. A remarkable painting, *On the Threshold*, 2010, depicts the artist blindfold, wearing a long black skirt and open green top; her hands are outstretched to feel the way as she stumbles forward in darkness. I am reminded of another, earlier, self-portrait by a woman artist that depicts a moment of personal transition, of indecision. The American Surrealist Dorothea Tanning's painting *Birthday*, 1942,[79] shows the artist, who is bare-breasted and wearing a long skirt overlaid with a tangle of thorns, standing in front of an endless succession of open doors that derive from the layout of her New York apartment. In Ghislaine's later depictions of a similar theme the familiar world of home and studio is also made strange, although here this results from her temporary blindness. Resolution lies within, in the heart, rather than within observable reality.

For Yeats, who wrote 'The Circus Animals' Desertion' shortly before his death in 1939, there was no real sense of resolution; he saw himself as 'a broken man' whose 'heart', the source of his poetry, is faltering and will soon be exhausted. Throughout his life he had consistently looked to a succession of women to provide him with the impetus to write, and who in turn inspired a sequence of visionary female figures who populated much of his earlier work. For all his uniqueness, in doing so Yeats was also living out a fairly conventional male artistic identity. Here, however, in *On the Threshold*, is a woman artist who, while acknowledging the role of the grand tradition, is also challenging it. The search for inner revelation is achieved by the very practical means of stumbling forward in the darkness; here, she has become her own muse.

The Circus Animals' Desertion

By William Butler Yeats

I

I sought a theme and sought for it in vain,
I sought it daily for six weeks or so.
Maybe at last being but a broken man
I must be satisfied with my heart, although
Winter and summer till old age began
My circus animals were all on show,
Those stilted boys, that burnished chariot,
Lion and woman and the Lord knows what.

II

What can I but enumerate old themes,
First that sea-rider Oisin led by the nose
Through three enchanted islands, allegorical dreams,
Vain gaiety, vain battle, vain repose,
Themes of the embittered heart, or so it seems,
That might adorn old songs or courtly shows;
But what cared I that set him on to ride,
I, starved for the bosom of his fairy bride.

And then a counter-truth filled out its play,
`The Countess Cathleen' was the name I gave it,
She, pity-crazed, had given her soul away
But masterful Heaven had intervened to save it.
I thought my dear must her own soul destroy
So did fanaticism and hate enslave it,
And this brought forth a dream and soon enough
This dream itself had all my thought and love.

And when the Fool and Blind Man stole the bread
Cuchulain fought the ungovernable sea;
Heart mysteries there, and yet when all is said
It was the dream itself enchanted me:
Character isolated by a deed
To engross the present and dominate memory.
Players and painted stage took all my love
And not those things that they were emblems of.

III

Those masterful images because complete
Grew in pure mind but out of what began?
A mound of refuse or the sweepings of a street,
Old kettles, old bottles, and a broken can,
Old iron, old bones, old rags, that raving slut
Who keeps the till. Now that my ladder's gone
I must lie down where all the ladders start
In the foul rag and bone shop of the heart.

Self-Portrait in the Studio
2010
Acrylic and sand on board
81.3 x 61 cm
Collect Art

Study for Self-Portrait in the Studio
(overleaf)
2010
Graphite and watercolour on paper
25.4 x 50.8 cm
Collection of the Artist

A blindfold can suggest many things: withdrawal, willed blindness, and the vulnerability of the fragile self unmasked. In this context it also suggests Ghislaine's need to keep a necessary distance between the herself and her work.

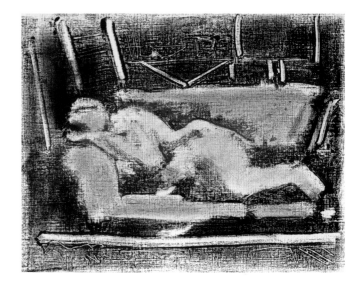

The Circus Animals'
Desertion
On the Sofa (I)
2010
Monotype with pastel
28 x 35.6 cm
Collection of the Artist

The Circus Animals'
Desertion
On the Sofa (II)
2010
Monotype with pastel
28 x 35.6 cm
Collection of the Artist

The Circus Animals'
Desertion
On the Sofa (III)
2010
Monotype with pastel
21 x 28 cm
Collection of the Artist

On the Threshold
(study)
2010
Oil on board
30.5 x 22.8 cm
Collection of the Artist

**Blindfolded Self-Portrait
with a Hand Mirror**
2010
Acrylic and pigment on board
61 x 61 cm
Collect Art

On the Threshold
(study)
2010
Oil on board
121.9 x 61 cm
Collect Art

**Blindfolded Self-Portrait
Holding the Mirror**
2010
Oil on board
15.25 x 20.3 cm
Collection of the Artist

On the Threshold
2010
Acrylic on board
91.4 x 61 cm
Private Collection

**Blindfolded Self-Portrait
with Chair**
2010
Acrylic on board
121.9 x 61 cm
Collection of the Artist

**The Circus Animals'
Desertion: Self-Portrait with
a Ladder**
2010
Monotype
10.2 x 15.25 cm
Collection of the Artist

**The Circus Animals'
Desertion: Holding the
Mirror**
2010
Monotype with pastel
10.2 x 15.25 cm
Collection of the Artist

**Blindfolded Self-Portrait
with Raised Arm**
2010
Monotype with pastel
28 x 21.6 cm
Collection of the Artist

**Tightrope Walker
Self-Portrait**
Oil on board
2010
15.25 x 20.3 cm
Collect Art

Henri Matisse likened himself to 'a dancer or tightrope walker who begins his day with several hours of numerous limbering exercises so that every part of his body obeys him'. In the same interview he compared his drawing to 'the gesture of a man groping his way in the darkness'.

Matisse, Le Point, no. 21, July 1939.

The Circus Animals' Desertion: Circus Horse Departing
Monotype with pastel
21 x 28 cm
Collection of the Artist

The Circus Animals' Desertion: Bareback Rider
2010
monotype
10.2 x 15.25 cm
Collection of the Artist

Tightrope Walker:
Self-Portrait
2010
Acrylic on board
61 x 91.4 cm
Collect Art

'Picasso had the Minotaur – I prefer the Centauress'

Ghislaine Howard

Centauress
2009
Monotype with pastel
19 x 24 cm
Collection of the Artist

11

Landscapes
The weather is king

Self-Portrait
Russell Road
1978
Acrylic on board
50.8 x 40.7 cm
Collection of the Artist

An open window is a powerful metaphor for the interplay between that which lies within and that which lies without. 'All that is asked is that we shall look for some time, in a special and undivided manner, at some simple, concrete and external thing,' the poet Evelyn Underhill suggested. 'This object of our contemplation may be almost anything we please: a picture, a statue, a tree, a distant hillside, a growing plant, little living things. ... Do not think, but as it were pour out your personality towards it: let your soul be in your eyes. Almost at once, this new method of perception will reveal unsuspected qualities in the external world.'[80]

A simple message, beautifully expressed, that may also be found in the writings of Blake, Wordsworth, Ruskin and later writers such as Ted Hughes and others; we are so used to projecting our needs and assorted desires onto the outside world that we rarely stop to allow ourselves to rest within nature and allow it to flood into us. Such opportunities do not only arise in rural or unspoilt panoramas, they can equally take us by surprise within the urban or suburban. Here is Baudelaire reminding his readers in 1846 that the modern city (in his case Paris) 'is rich in poetic and wonderful subjects. The marvellous envelops and saturates us like the atmosphere, but we fail to see it.' And of course, if we look up from whatever landscape we are in, there is the sky; the 'great skies that let one dream of eternity'.[81]

Painting the landscape of any kind can bring a breath of fresh air into

studio practice and renew a sense of connectivity with the outside world. Though she is primarily a figurative painter, seascapes, landscapes and cityscapes appear at unprogrammed intervals throughout Ghislaine's work, and over the years she has produced a large body of work inspired by her surroundings, the places she has lived and those that she has visited either to seek out specific landscapes painted by the artists she admires or quite simply as part of a holiday experience. However, our move to Glossop in 1985 caused a shift of emphasis, for Ghislaine had known this landscape from childhood trips with her family and later as home to friends whom we would visit. Walking our dogs in all weathers, we grew ever more familiar with the fields and valleys, hills and moorlands of Glossopdale and soon the imposing rock formations of the Wormstones, Cown Edge, Crowden and the bleak grandeur of Snake Summit began to appear in her paintings.

It is an ancient landscape that was once covered in mixed woodland, deforested during the Bronze and Iron Ages, and has been open moorland only since Roman times. It is a place of sudden contrasts. At one turn nature seems to leap out of the void and overwhelm the walker with a sudden rise or fall of rock; another turn reveals a flowing vista of rounded hills, folding away into the distance and always keeping us company, the silhouettes of broken stone, etched against an ever-changing sky. Ghislaine feels a particular affinity with the austere beauty of this landscape, so much of it endowed with evocative names and all of which

Cliffs at Flamborough Head
1990
Oil on canvas
71 x 147.3 cm
Collection of the Artist

'Manchester is a city of chaos and commotion, of commerce and creativity, of machines and music. Ghislaine's bold staccato brushwork evokes this vital thrumming energy, a mental snapshot from a moving train. Approaching Piccadilly captures the moment when the long evening light crosses the Cheshire plains and hits the gap-toothed skyline creating an urban diorama as colourful as a rain forest.'

Thom Hetherington
Director, Buy Art Fair and The Manchester Contemporary

Approaching Piccadilly Station
2016
Oil on board
61 x 152.4 cm
Collect Art

Beetham Tower, Manchester
2014
Oil on board
22.8 x 30.5 cm
Private Collection

The Grain Elevator No 2
(opposite)
1983
Oil on board
15.25 x 22.8cm
Private Collection

lie within a short distance from our home, and it has become an active and shaping presence in her life.

She records her impressions in sketchbooks, depicting the essential features of things seen in rapid notational jottings, which sometimes seem to be more like pieces of calligraphy than drawing. These may become works in their own right or documents full of information, crystallisations of complex forms that can become the starting point for more considered works. But it is also a discipline in itself: hand, eye and mind working in accord with the body.

Rising from the Cheshire plain and receiving the afternoon light from the west, Glossopdale is characterised by dramatic shifts of weather and light – nothing remains fixed or stable for long. Its rich textures and muted colours can in an instant, be brought to life by a sudden flash of light, transforming the sombre ochres into burning gold and dull greys into shimmering silver and then an unexpected sweep of rain or mist might obliterate everything from view, for in this landscape the weather is king. Such experiences go right to the heart of what it is to be in the world,

and it is significant that this landscape was home to one of the greatest philosophers of the last century, Ludwig Wittgenstein. As a young man, he spent time on the moors above Glossop and he got to know them intimately. His knowledge of this landscape and others that he sought out throughout his life, coloured much of his thinking.

He wrote that a philosophical problem is like being lost, for one can see but not know where one is – and so understanding is about recognising certain significant landmarks and allowing oneself to 'place' oneself within the landscape – a sense of being at home. Surely this is one of the key aspects of landscape painting – to make the world visible, to map it and give it order. Lowry, who lived on the edge of the Peak District and knew Glossop and its surrounding landscape well, understood this and perversely painted it as the most *unheimlich*, of places – forbidding and unwelcoming, the very antithesis of the security we associate with home. There are times, walking back home with our dog, that we have cast a backward glance at the hills and in doing so catch the landscape taking on a different persona in the fading light, and wonder at our audacity in intruding upon such an alien territory.

Time passes and I turn towards home,
Cast a backward look at the shrouded slab of darkness,
Sullen now against the curtain sky,
It offers no invitation to roam.[82]

Ghislaine has a great sense of the variety and relatedness of things. She brings them together, gives them unity, a sense of wholeness and vitality – as she does with her paintings of the figure. The great landscape painters and poets of China knew that there is a close correlation between the structures of the human body and those of the landscape as did Leonardo da Vinci. This is something Ghislaine feels instinctively, to such an extent that some of her landscapes could be mistaken for studies of the human form and vice versa. Looking upon the Derbyshire landscape, this is not as fanciful as it might seem. This is partly because Ghislaine brings her landscapes up close; she has little time for traditional models of perspective that sets it into a neat box and gives it a sense of spurious order. Instead, she lets her eye meander until it fixes upon a key moment in the landscape, a rock formation perhaps, or a particular conjuncture of land and sky and then that point becomes the fulcrum of the composition. It is the artist who brings this into some kind of ordering, or better, who reveals the often hidden structures that underlie the 'superficial' aspects of the terrain and brings them together, the land and the sky, or in a seascape, sea, sky and land.

The painting, when finished, is an invitation to voyage – to enter into it on an imaginary journey as one might move through the geography of a real landscape. And, as in a real landscape, there must always be a certain amount of indeterminacy, and of course, some things aren't seen at all; they can only be guessed at, imagined, as in a Japanese zen garden – this sparks our curiosity and we want to know more. Uncertainty is an essential part of our local landscape where a sudden fall of cloud or a sheet of rain can completely change our experience of our immediate surroundings, sometimes rendering it completely invisible. Such energies are larger than us and they call for respect, and so, while Ghislaine's landscapes carry no overt environmental message, nevertheless she gives an unsentimental view of those forces, human or natural, that shape our land, town, city and seascapes and sends us back to them with fresh eyes, reinvigorated.

Saltwick Nab
1990
Oil on canvas
127 x 101.6 cm
Collection of the Artist

On occasion, inspired by the scholar painters of China, she takes long rolls of heavy-duty lining paper that can be weighted down with rocks and worked on in situ. These can be up to 15 feet in length and allow her to respond to the landscape unfettered by the predetermined format of sketchbook or canvas edge.

Despite recent developments, Glossop still has the look of a Victorian mill town with evidence of the tumultuous changes that took place during that period – the mills, now turned to other uses, terraced streets, parks and impressive civic buildings. As Turner and Constable painted the beginnings of the Industrial Revolution and as Lowry marked its terminal decline, like them Ghislaine rejects the picturesque and seeks out the weighty underlying structures that are themselves subject to the first law of evolution: constant change.

It is such qualities that Ghislaine's paintings suggest. She is neither a philosopher, a geologist nor an academic, but an artist, a wanderer, who tries in her works to allow the landscape to reveal itself, rather than to impose a certain order upon it. For we are within life, not outside it, and this is what Ghislaine seeks to express. Her approach to landscape painting is as direct as her approach to her figurative work. There have been shifts in her style of painting over the years, but her landscapes have always been marked by forceful brushwork that follow the structures of the forms before her, charting those elements with broad passages of colour roughly laid down that signal not only the structure but also the look of the landscape. Her colours do not necessarily describe, but evoke time, place and space – the conjunction of the elements – air, sea and rock, referencing both the power of the motif and the material reality of the painted surface. It is a vigorous and expressive way of painting. These works are normally painted swiftly, but may take any amount of time to complete, each mark recording the physical and mental energy that it takes to hit the right colours, the right marks and to weave them into the developing totality of the painting.

It is a simple matter in theory to take out into the landscape basic drawing and painting materials, but quite another in practice. Ghislaine's preferred method is to make rapid brush drawings on the spot, weather permitting,

with colour added either then or on returning to the studio. Sometimes she takes out small panels and a limited number of paints, and works directly from her chosen motif. Sometimes, following Turner's practice, she carries with her into the landscape small rolls or folds of paper that can be unscrolled to correspond to the panorama that lies before her. On occasion, inspired by the scholar painters of China, she takes long rolls of heavy-duty lining paper that can be weighted down with rocks and worked on in situ. These can be up to 15 feet in length and allow her to respond to the landscape unfettered by the predetermined format of sketchbook or canvas edge.

Out in the open air, surrounded by the elements and armed only with brush, panels or paper, there is often no time to consider the impossibility of the task in hand; the process is not describing the landscape but responding to it, allowing for accidents to happen whilst working at a pitch of concentration that, it is hoped, will result in something worthwhile. On the beach it can be particles of sand blown onto the canvas, on the hills a sudden flurry of rain but all this is to be welcomed as they set into the painting hard material evidence of the actuality of the painting's genesis – a record of engagement with the world, rather a picture of it. So landscape painting, far from being a conservative genre, is potentially one of the most radical – it can help us to understand how we think of nature and culture, society and ecology, object and meaning.

It is a way of entering into sympathy with the world – whether it's the human or natural landscape – to do justice to what connects us to the world and what it is that causes us to feel a certain separateness from it too. Something felt most intently by Lowry: 'It's so simple to set down in words, and yet so fiendishly complicated to achieve in paint – how do you capture what's out there, and why? and for what purpose?'[83]

Ghislaine is an intensely physical painter, the gestures and movements of her body are an active part of the creation of the painting. This is very effective in figure painting, but she carries it through to her landscape work which is perhaps why Sister Wendy Beckett referred to her as an 'erotic painter'.

Cliffs at Houlgate
1990
Oil on flax
50.8 x 61 cm
Collect Art

Cleft in the Rocks Flamborough Head
(opposite) 1990
Oil on board
83.8 x 58.4 cm
Collect Art

'There is energy, excess and a kind of muscularity in her canvases, untainted by cynicism and art circuit chic. Ghislaine Howard paints directly, sometimes furiously, attacking both subject and canvas with a passion for her colours and her craft. The massiveness of rocks, the swell of the sea and the tints of stormy skies are all translated into the stuff of paint, in a way that sometimes suggests late Bomberg.'

Richard Kendall, author of Degas by Himself.

Cliff near St. Davids
2014
Acrylic on panel
10 x 25.4 cm
Collect Art

Pentre Ifan
1990
Acrylic on board
22.8 x 30.5 cm
Collection of the Artist

Sea and Rocks, Staithes
2015
Acrylic on board
20.3 x 15.25 cm
Collect Art

Poppit Sands
2015
Acrylic on board
22.8 x 30.5 cm
Collect Art

Ghislaine is an intensely physical painter, the gestures and movements of her body are an active part of the creation of the painting; the sweep of the arm and the more delicate or determined movements of hand and wrist – these large movements are evidenced in the marks left on the canvas that carry the rhythm and heft of bodily gesture. This is a powerful visualising agency, the marks having a direct correlation with the physical actions of the painter. This is very effective in figure painting, but she carries it through to her landscape work which is perhaps why Sister Wendy Beckett referred to her as an 'erotic painter'.[84]

Ingres once said about the anatomy, 'I do not know the names of the bones that make up the human body, but they are all my friends.' The same applies to landscape; to recognise and love the shift of terrain, its openings, folds and enclosures – the slow rise and sudden fall, the great sweep of a panoramic view and the abruptness of a quarry wall.

So many of these ideas find a resonance in Joachim Gasquet's account of a meeting with Cézanne in which the artist explained: '"I have my motif" ... He clasps his hands together ... He repeats his gesture, separates his hands, spreading his fingers apart, and brings them slowly, very slowly together again, then joins them, clenches them, intertwining his fingers. "That's what you have to attain. ... Nature is always the same, but nothing about her that we see endures. Our art must convey a glimmer of her endurance with the elements, the appearance of all her changes. It must

give us the sense of her eternity. What is beneath her? Perhaps nothing. Perhaps everything. Everything, you understand? So, I join her wandering hands ..."'[85]

There it is, the challenge is to paint with the same energy and 'logic' of that understanding, that revelation, to allow the composition, the paint, the charcoal lines to weave together in accordance to the rhythms and forces of the natural world. To make an object in 'correspondence' with the motif and to capture something something that Emmanuel Levinas called the 'very strangeness of the earth'.[86]

Though we live in landlocked Derbyshire, the sea is not too far away and one of the many sources of the River Mersey springs out of the moors a few miles away from our home. This water passes by our house and eventually flows past the docks where my father worked in Liverpool. The call of the sea is irresistible – for us as it was for Lowry. Like him, we relish the shock of its rolling distances, the play of the great maritime clouds and its endless mutability. It's one of the great subjects: the impressive reach of the waves, the crystalline light, so different from the defused opalescent light of the hills we know so well. Looking towards the horizon, we are drawn to consider the space between what we know and what we feel. But whatever the motif, whatever the subject of the artist's gaze, the challenge remains the same. Not to represent what the landscape looks like, but to evoke the energies that give it form.

**Seen from the Train
Queensland**
2014
Acrylic on board
20.3 x 15.25 cm
Collection of the Artist

However, we need only experience walking the high moors amongst the low lying clouds to recognise a kinship of sorts with Ludwig Wittgenstein. He trod these same pathways, broke cover and tramped across the springy heather and exposed peat, leapt over the deep blackness of half-hidden cloughs. He would have marvelled and been troubled by the ever-shifting shapes, colours, sounds and smells that assailed his quickened senses.

During the last 18 months of his life, Wittgenstein set down his 'Remarks On Colour'.[87] It would be foolish to suggest that the impact of the tawny landscape around Chunal had any direct contribution upon such a late production, but nevertheless many of his thoughts echo those inspired by any walker in open country as the landscape shifts and changes with the light and weather.

View from the Kitchen Glossop
(opposite)
2015
Oil on board
15.25 x 20.3 cm
Collect Art

Moor above Glossop I
2013
Monoprint with pastel
7.6 x 22.8
Collection of the Artist

Moor above Glossop II
2013
Monoprint with pastel
7.6 x 22.8
Collection of the Artist

Moor above Glossop III
2013
Monoprint with pastel
7.6 x 22.8
Collection of the Artist

Moor above Glossop IIII
2013
Monoprint with pastel
7.6 x 22.8
Collection of the Artist

'The Idea of Order at Key West'

She was the single artificer of the world
In which she sang. And when she sang, the sea,
Whatever self it had, became the self
That was her song, for she was the maker.
Then we,
As we beheld her striding there alone,
Knew that there never was a world for her
Except the one she sang and, singing, made.

Wallace Stevens

Woman by the Waves
2013
Acrylic on board
58.42 x 88.9 cm
Courtesy of Gateway Gallery

12

Choreography of Walking
Everything we ever do begins with our first step

Despite everything, we are still nomadic creatures. Walking, like breathing, is fundamental to life – to be able to move towards food, away from danger or simply to get from here to there. And to watch the human body in movement is a compelling activity – for everyone's walk is different.

Ghislaine has drawn figures and animals in movement all her life. There is such a simple pleasure in watching people and attempting to catch something of their distinctive gait. The birth of Max spurred her into a very intimate engagement with every moment of his development, from his initial uncoordinated movements to his first hesitant steps and beyond. She kept a close watch on both our children as they grew and has witnessed the determination and courage of her mother refusing to accept the debilitating progress of Parkinson's disease. Such personal experiences have chimed with the depictions of walking that we have come to love, and from which Ghislaine has learnt so much: the earthy weight of Giotto's figures, those of Masaccio, Rembrandt, Delacroix, Rodin and not least Muybridge's extraordinary photographs of humans and animals in motion. The list is endless, but one stands out, from the crowd, so to speak: Goya's almost unbearably poignant drawing of himself in old age. He imagines himself as a crippled beggar, walking with two sticks out of the darkness into the light. Written on the drawing are two words: 'Aun Aprendo' ('Still Learning').

Walking plays such a large role in our history and culture – think of the importance of walking in religion, myth and legend, the solitary wandering of Jesus and Buddha to gain enlightenment, Christ's journey to the Cross, for example, and in our modern age, Baudelaire's fascination with the flâneur, the Situationists' theory of Psychogeography and artists such as Giacometti, Richard Long and of course, L. S. Lowry.

In October 2009, Ghislaine began an informal working relationship with the Podiatry department at Salford University. It was a marvellous opportunity to underpin her understanding of the mechanics of walking by working with the staff and students, attending anatomy classes and making studies in the Gait Measuring Laboratory where computer generated images and video footage are used to analyse every aspect of each individual patient's gait. She mostly worked with children with cerebral palsy; she would draw them as they moved between two fixed points. There was something compelling and humbling to watch and chart these short challenging journeys.

I made drawings as they were being examined by the physiotherapist and then as they walked repeatedly between two fixed points in the Gait Measuring Laboratory. I was drawn to the extraordinary choreography of these short journeys, the determination of each child and the support of their

families. The drawings also chart an exciting interaction between the oldest of technologies – making marks on paper or canvas with pigment, and the latest computer generated data and imagery.

This experience was just one aspect of her fascination with walking. In recent years, she has made many studies of her mother as she pushed her weakening body to its very limits in her determination to keep walking. Ghislaine has made numerous canvases, prints and drawings of her mother's distinctive, almost dance-like gait, despite the effects of Parkinson's disease, she made her way through the spaces of her house.

It is ironic, perhaps, that early in her career, Ghislaine went into institutions in order to study the extremes of life and now, decades later, she has found them, and charted them within her own domestic milieu.

Gait Lab Study
Young Boy in Movement
(left)
2010
Ink on paper
25.4 x 25.4 cm
Collect Art

My Mother Walking
2008
Graphite on paper
25.4 x 17.8 cm
Collection of the Artist

Movement Study (I)
Monotype
2010
43.2 x 33 cm
Collect Art

Movement Study (II)
Monotype
2010
43.2 x 33 cm
Collect Art

Movement Study (III)
Monotype
2010
43.2 x 33 cm
Collect Art

Young Man Walking
2009
Acrylic on board
91.4 x 61 cm
Collect Art

Walking Figure, Glossop
2009
Oil on board
20.3 x 15.25 cm
Collect Art

Young Man in Headphones
2016
Oil on board
122 x 61 cm
Private Collection
Photograph Art Decor Gallery

My Mother Walking
(triptych)
2008
Oil on board
182.9 x 91.4 cm
Collect Art

**My Mother Reaching into
her Wardrobe**
(opposite)
2010
Acrylic on board
61 x 61 cm
Collection of the Artist

13

Seven Acts of Mercy
Compassion and empathy

After Caravaggio's
Seven Works of Mercy
(1607)
2014
Oil on canvas
127 x 101.6 cm
Private Collection

During a New Year visit to Madrid in 2012 we saw and were deeply moved by two small medieval panels relating to the Seven Acts of Mercy. Later, as we talked over coffee, we discussed the eloquence of their simple compositions and the power and relevance of their subject matter, for this simple idea, Seven Works of Mercy, is not just an idea, but an injunction to act. The actions they reference are central to any humane and caring society and, though specifically Christian in this form, the ideas they embody are set at the heart of all the world's major religions.

To feed the hungry
To give drink to the thirsty
To clothe the naked
To house the homeless
To visit the sick
To visit the prisoner
To bury the dead

Ghislaine realised: *that the absence or presence of these ideas had been the unacknowledged guiding principle behind my 365 Series, so a few years ago, I began to seek out contemporary images relating to them in a more direct way with the intention of using them as a catalyst for seven major canvases, each relating in some way to one of the Acts of Mercy. Separately and as a*

group I want them to speak of this powerful and universal theme: what we share as human beings – our capacity for empathy and compassion as well as our capacity to inflict violence and create suffering.

These small panels have been used in various ways. Gathered into sets of seven, each panel relating to one of the Seven Acts of Mercy, they have been given to different groups who can respond and reflect upon their significance, discuss and share their thoughts and feelings before passing them on to another community. They have been used in this way by gallery visitors, different faith groups, and college and school children with startling results as individuals and groups from a variety of different social, ethnic and cultural backgrounds exchange panels and in doing so, share memories, stories and prejudices. The panels operate silently and in bypassing the intrusiveness of language, self-reflection and interpretation become more possible. The recipient handles what is evidently a work of art, hand-crafted, but one that is also an object that can be dropped like any other. Passed from hand to hand in this way they take on the nature of a gift, bestowed from one to another. This transaction seems to touch something deep within human nature, which is to be grateful for something freely given and to want to offer something in return. Thus, a communion is made easier and in that process people talk – it's as simple as that. The project is still developing, but already there have been some wonderful results, both here and abroad.

Tony Marshall is head teacher of Oude Molen school in Cape Town where seven of the panels have been placed. He described in a letter how the panels are used:

> Understated in their size and colouring, to me they reflect
> the way good can be done without celebrity or fanfare,
> the panels are a constant reminder of the reasons our

'I am reminded that education is not merely about certificates but is about role models of ways of being.'

Tony Marshall. Cape Town

Welcome the Stranger
(study)
2016
Oil on board
61 x 91.4 cm
Collection of the Artist

school opened its doors to all for the first time in 1990. And they invite a continuing holistic response. Oude Molen is a school populated almost exclusively by the children of previously disenfranchised parents and now often economically disadvantaged because of the legacy of apartheid education, and I am reminded that education is not merely about certificates but is about role models of ways of being. Our School Management Team shares my experience of the panels and invites others to recognise our privilege and responsibility for each other's well-being. Then to find a way to live compassionately, sharing each other's burdens.[88]

This letter confirms a belief that runs like a thread through the narrative of Ghislaine's art, this book and our lives. It is simply this: that art should, where it can, operate as a force for the good and that it should be part of life and not apart from it. It can be a visualisation of the very best, and the very worst, of what we are – a parallel discourse that links with language and the daily reality of life itself, public and private and the spaces where those two extremes mingle and touch.

Around the time we received this message from Tony Marshall, Chris Evans, a friend of Ghislaine's from her schooldays, told her of a newspaper article she had read that had touched her deeply. We haven't checked the exact facts of this report, because stories have their own truths that

Give Food to the Hungry
(study)
2013
Oil and pigment on flax
127 x 101.6 cm
Collection of the Artist

shift and change in the telling but, as we remember it, the report centred upon a young woman who was describing her experience as she travelled in the funeral cortège that was taking her father to his final resting place. The city streets were full of people, each preoccupied with their own business, oblivious to her situation. Sitting in the limousine, she felt completely alone in her grief, numb and lost. And then, just as they were passing a greengrocer's stall, she noticed a young man in a hoodie, who stopped serving his customer, set down the paper bag he was holding and stood with hands clasped and head bowed as the cortège passed, before returning to finish the transaction. A simple act of respect that helped the young woman to feel less alone in the world and more able to make sense of her sorrow. These ideas and her experience of painting the 365 panels have inspired Ghislaine to begin work on a series of seven major canvases each of which will be dedicated to one of the Acts of Mercy. The curator Lesley Sutton featured a number of studies for these at the first PassionArt Trail exhibition of 2014, where they were shown at Saint Ann's Church in Manchester city centre.

Lesley wrote of her first glimpse of the large study, *Give Drink to the Thirsty*:

> I first saw this painting, unfinished, taped to the wall of the former school art room which now serves as Ghislaine's studio. The whole space was filled with canvases, paintings and sketches stacked against walls and on table tops, the smell of paint accompanying the nostalgic scent of school corridors. The room was filled with an immense sense of energy. Ghislaine's enthusiasm for life and her compassion towards people is contagious and there, captured through vivid colour and broad brushstrokes were the raw and honest emotions that make us human. But the deep cobalt blue of this one painting kept calling me towards the far wall where, in this simple act of the passing of a glass of water, I could recognise and feel a sense of awkwardness and hesitancy within myself as I identified with both the giver and receiver; a sense of unworthiness even, and a troubling reluctance to trust a fellow human being. For myself particularly, a certain uncomfortableness with the gift of grace when it is materially given; my fear of giving away love in case it is rejected.

> 'As I drew closer, I became more aware of Ghislaine's ability to respond to the subtle gestures we make in our everyday lives, how the unspoken language of the body is loaded with tension and grace that express the paradox that is the human condition: our longing for love, compassion, beauty and generosity going hand in hand with our overwhelming tendency to fear, judge and hate. Her work examines our conscience. How do I choose to live today?'[89]

Give Drink to the Thirsty
(previous)
2013
Acrylic and pigment on linen
155 x 182.9 cm
Collection of the Artist

**The Return of the Prodigal
Son**
(study)
2013
Acrylic on canvas
61 x 61cm
Collection of the Artist

As ever, one thing sparks another and when in 2014, Ghislaine was asked
to produce work for an exhibition in Saint Ann's church in Manchester
city centre, she decided to exhibit some of the studies for the Seven Acts
and to produce a major work especially for the occasion, *The Return
of the Prodigal Son*. The Nigerian novelist, Ben Okri has written, 'The
parables of Jesus are more powerful than his miracles',[90] and the parable in
which all the Seven Acts find a home is surely that of the Prodigal Son. It
was a subject entirely fitting for that particular church as it is one in which
many vulnerable people find a haven. In taking this subject, Ghislaine
was aware of the immensity of the task for both Rembrandt in his late
canvas of c.1662 and the Russian film-maker Andrei Tarkovsky in his
1972 film, *Solaris*, have given quintessential renderings of this subject.[91]
However, undeterred by the sublime achievement of these works,
Ghislaine set herself to reaffirm the themes of home, memory, love, loss
and redemption that are central to its narrative.

**The Return of the Prodigal
Son**
(opposite)
2014
Acrylic on canvas
243.9 x 182.9 cm
Collection of the Artist

END PIECE

An Archaeologist's Appreciation

Jill Cook
The British Museum, August, 2016

It is a rare privilege for an archaeologist and museum curator to have the opportunity to express her debt to an artist in a book about her. The background to this requires a little preliminary digression to explain how Ghislaine Howard's distinctive work began to touch my own life and enrich my research.

One day in an undergraduate archaeology class a lecturer momentarily showed a slide of a small, 24,000-year-old limestone sculpture of a woman and passed on with the words, 'and we all know what Palaeolithic men were thinking about when they made this'. The image was of the figure from Willendorf, Austria, referred to by the misnomer 'Venus' because of the supposed savage eroticism of her full figure and nudity. I was dismayed by the assumptions and such rapid, prejudiced dismissal of an ancient work of art. Dismay quickly translated into fascination and curiosity. I have been researching images of women in 40,000 to 10,000-year-old Ice Age art ever since and acknowledge my discovery of Ghislaine's charcoal drawing of *Pregnant Self-Portrait*, 1987 as a turning point almost every day. I first saw the drawing in 1991 at the Whitworth Art Gallery, Manchester in an exhibition called 'Women and Men' in which works were shown in pairs, one by a man

and one by a woman.[92] Once the visitors had responded in their own way to the images, they could lift a flap covering the label to discover the gender of the artist. Ghislaine's charcoal drawing of herself pregnant was paired with Jacob Epstein's large marble sculpture *Genesis*, 1930. The clever juxtaposition of these two responses to pregnancy crystallized and reinforced so much of my thinking about ways of seeing female images from the Ice Age, many of which are shown in various stages of pregnancy and giving birth. Whereas *Pregnant Self-Portrait*, 1987 reveals a personal, calm, tender expression of the body's physical change and the strange, wondrous feelings of the first stirrings of life inside, Epstein's grandiose attempt to represent the origins of humanity is distanced as allegory necessitated by the absence of direct personal experience. The contrast between the images created by male and female artists, as well as the perspective, posture and gaze of Ghislaine's self-portrait and those of other expectant mothers produced while she was artist in residence at St Mary's Hospital in Manchester, gave me a new visual reference when looking at Ice Age representations.

As I began to interpret the modest Ice Age figures, I saw the same personal intimacy and

informality in the expression of the female body as in Ghislaine's work. At about the same time a colleague, obstetrician Jean-Pierre Duhard medicalised archaeological thinking by identifying the physiological characteristics of each trimester of pregnancy in the French pieces but, out of a supposed duty to objectivity, stopped short of suggesting that they might be objects made by, for and about women. The British Museum exhibition 'Ice Age art: arrival of the modern mind' in 2013 provided an opportunity to offer this possibility to the public.

Pregnant Self-Portrait, 1987 was at the top of my loan list for the exhibition which included works by twentieth-century artists in order to bring our own capabilities and experiences into the same orbit as those of the distant past made by people like us in every way except their way of life. Evaluations of the exhibition revealed that some people felt they had not needed Moore, Matisse and Picasso to break the time barrier and help them connect. By contrast many remarked that they were moved by the juxtaposition of Ghislaine's compelling work. Its scale and view of the female body, as well as the use of charcoal, a delicate, impermanent medium frequently used by Ice Age artists, gave a touching sense of connection and experience

translating the imagery into an eternal present. Like the stone and ivory sculptures of 30,000–20,000 years ago, *Pregnant Self-Portrait* embodies female experience and kinship, giving exquisite expression to feelings beyond words needing no explanation in a label.

In the year after 'Ice Age art' at the British Museum, Ghislaine generously supported a much smaller show in the temporary gallery space at the Creswell Crags Museum and Visitor Centre situated amongst the caves on the Nottinghamshire/Derbyshire border in which the few pieces of Ice Age art from Britain were found. The exhibition explored the visual context of a small engraved drawing of a male figure with an erect penis and animal head inscribed on the fossilized rib bone of a woolly rhinoceros about 13,500 years ago. The addition of Ghislaine's elemental ink drawings of male figures again provoked new ways of

looking, seeing and thinking about drawing, the human body and our relationships with art and the past.

Over nearly twenty years, I have included Ghislaine's drawing in lectures, and display a postcard of it on my desk. In archaeology, as in art, it reflects a rebalancing of the male dominated view. This has touched me again in Ghislaine's *365 series* in which her simply expressive paintings again give voice to the feelings that silence and overwhelm us in the content of daily media news coverage.

I discovered this deeply moving series after I commissioned Francesco Tuccio, the carpenter of Lampedusa, to make a cross for the British Museum from the wreckage of a refugee boat like those he makes for the refugees rescued by the islanders, in order to express empathy for them and hope for their future. The

commission was inspired by a media report and, like Ghislaine's *365 series,* was made as a gesture to record that although disempowered by overwhelming, apparently unstoppable political process, people still feel for and care about the desperate plights of others.

Ghislaine and I have not met so I am all the more delighted to have the opportunity to offer this appreciation of her work that communicates such a humane expression of our times with great generosity of spirit and simple beauty. Her subjects seem to find her so naturally that her gift for drawing distils and preserves their meaning. As our times pass into history, I think that her consummate artistic skill will come to be acknowledged as among the greatest of our times.

Pregnant Self-Portrait
(opposite)
1987
Charcoal on paper
75.8 x 55.9 cm
Collection of the Whitworth Art
Gallery, Manchester
© Whitworth Art Gallery

A Heavily Pregnant Woman
(From Kostienki 1, Russia)
c. 22,000 BCE
Limestone
13.5 cm
Courtesy of Kunstkamera
Saint Petersburg

Ghislaine in the Studio, Glossop
(previous)
2016
Photograph by Adrian Lambert

Footnotes

1. Emily Dickinson, letter to Thomas Wentworth Higginson, 1870, L342a.
2. A. J. ('Con') Leventhal, 'The Thirties', *Beckett at Sixty*, Calder and Boyars, 1967, p.7.
3. *The Condition of the Working Class in England* was written between 1844–5, but only published in England in 1891.
4. In a recent radio broadcast, David Hockney recounted that the very same Van Gogh image had helped pull him out of a prolonged period of depression and inspired him into a renewed period of creative activity.
5. Marcel Proust's great novel, *À la recherche du temps perdu*, (1913–27) has been translated into English twice – as *Remembrance of Things Past* and as *In Search of Lost Time*.
6. Ghislaine's words echo those of the Swedish film director Ingmar Bergman describing his response to seeing the films of Andrei Tarkovsky. 'Suddenly, I found myself standing at the door of a room, the keys of which had, until then, never been given to me. It was a room I had always wanted to enter and where he was moving freely and fully at ease. I felt encouraged and stimulated: someone was expressing what I had always wanted to say without knowing how. Tarkovsky is for me the greatest, the one who invented a new language, true to the nature of film, as it captures life as a reflection, life as a dream.' This has been quoted many times, 'Ingmar Bergman Evaluates His Fellow Filmmakers – The "Affected" Godard, "Infantile" Hitchcock & Sublime Tarkovsky', in *Film*, 18 October 2013.
7. John T. Irwin, *Scott Fitzgerald's Fiction, An Almost Theatrical Innocence*, John Hopkins University Press, 2014, p.ix.
8. Our daughter Cordelia still wears one of these, as she reminded us when helping us edit this book.
9. For me, Chartiers had another association: it was in a room immediately above the restaurant that Isidore-Lucien Ducasse, the self-styled Comte de Lautréamont and author of *Les Chants du Maldoror*, died in 1870, aged 24.
10. Adolphe Valette (1876–1942) was a French painter who taught at Manchester School of Art from 1906 to1920. He had a powerful and lasting influence on L. S. Lowry; see my *L. S. Lowry: A Visionary Artist*, Lowry Press, 2000. For a brief period, Valette produced a number of evocative paintings of the city, in which its polluted atmosphere became the very means to transform its streets, canals and buildings into a site/sight of unexpected beauty.
11. In 1964, an exhibition at Monks Hall Museum in Eccles was organised to celebrate L. S. Lowry's 77th birthday. His work was shown there together with that of 25 contemporary artists including Dame Barbara Hepworth, Henry Moore, Victor Pasmore and Ivon Hitchens, all of whom submitted works in honour of his achievement. Sir Kenneth Clark, Jacob Bronowski and others contributed written appreciations.
12. A term used to denote painters whose technical prowess and sensitivity towards their medium make them a model for other painters.
13. Jim Aulich, *City Life*, 3 May 1985.
14. Piero's imperious Madonna stands, heavily pregnant, her right hand drawing attention to her blue dress which opens to reveal a shock of white undergarment. *Madonna del Parto* translates as 'Madonna of Childbirth'.
15. Michael Ayrton, *Rudiments of Paradise*, Secker & Warburg, 1970, pp.27–31.
16. 'You're' was included in Sylvia Plath's second collection of poems, *Ariel*, first published in1965.
17. Avigdor Arikha (1929–2010), Israeli painter, draughtsman, printmaker and author of *On Depiction,* Bellew Publishing, 1995.
18. Jane Fickling, *The Daily Telegraph*, 29 January 1993.
19. Antonina Vallentin, *Picasso*, Cassell, 1963, (first published 1957), p.168.
20. As reported by the Irish writer, George Moore in 'Degas: The Painter of Modern Life.' *Magazine of Art* 13 (October 1890), pp.416–25.
21. *Degas and the Dance* (PBS; BBC; Arte; NHK) (2003), directed by Mischa Scorer. Winner of 2004 Peabody Award; Cine Golden Eagle Award 2004; Grand Prix de L'Image, Fifart (Unesco) 2005.
22. Ghislaine's features are indeed similar to those found in Lowry's paintings of his purported godchild, Ann Hilder, that he produced in his later years. Despite extensive research, it has, as yet, proved impossible to confirm the existence or identity of Ann. She was probably an imaginary figure based on the young friends he knew, although those who heard him speak of her never doubted the actuality of her existence.
23. Frank Cohen, a passionate collector of art is responsible for this wonderful nugget of information. As he tells it, 'I was in a restaurant in London a few years ago with my wife, and Lucian Freud was sitting in the corner. We started talking and I asked him who he liked as an artist. He said "Auerbach and Lowry" and I couldn't believe it, I really was amazed. He said he was a fantastic artist and he loved him. There you are – from Freud's own mouth.' Collector Frank Cohen Remembers L. S. Lowry', Sotheby's website, 10 Nov 2015 www. sothebys.com/en/news-video/blogs/all.../collector-frank-cohen-ls-lowry.html**.** Frank Auerbach also 'rates' L. S. Lowry, as he makes clear in the recent publication, *Frank Auerbach: Speaking and Painting*, Catherine Lambert, Thames & Hudson, 2015, p.76. We should also mention Paula Rego who in 2014, in conversation with Robert McPherson, told of her admiration for Lowry – as a man and a teacher as well as for the quality of his work, 'some pictures are really beautiful and wonderful.'
24. In 1863, the poet and critic Charles Baudelaire wrote an essay, 'The Painter of Modern Life', a piece of writing that inspired the Impressionists and has remained a challenge for serious artists ever since. The essay is a clarion call for a painter who would be able to extract 'the eternal and the immutable' from the 'the ephemeral, the fugitive, and the contingent' qualities that he saw as the essential characteristics of contemporary experience.
25. Ghislaine was unaware at this time of Barbara Hepworth's remarkable series of drawings and paintings that she produced during the late 1940s that show hospital surgeons at work. Similar in subject they may be, but the interpretation of medical intervention could hardly be more different.
26. Jane Fickling, *The Daily Telegraph*, 29 January 1993.
27. Robert Clark, *The Guardian*, 29 March1993.
28. Hans Arp, *On My Way, Poetry and Essays 1912–1947*, Wittenborn, Schultz, 1948, p. 39, as quoted in Michael Howard and Debbie Lewer, *A New Order: An Evening at the Cabaret Voltaire*, Manchester Metropolitan University, 1995, p.46. The performance team for 'A New Order: An Evening at the Cabaret Voltaire' included: Sarah-Jane Field, Denis Herdman, Colette Murray, Dave Mahoney, Alex Whitham, Ian Tate and Jane Bedford, as well as students from the School of Interactive Arts at MMU. The production won the Manchester Evening News Theatre Award for 'Best of the Fringe'.
29. Communication with the artist (undated). In 2004 Ghislaine was approached to produce a miniature version of the *Stations of the Cross / The Captive Figure* for a chapel dedicated to those bereaved by suicide in Nottingham. At first she thought this an impossible commission but on completing the series, she realised that small paintings can have as much emotional power as large-scale works – an idea that informed much of her later practice, including the *365 Series* of daily paintings, her transcriptions after Goya, and many of her domestic paintings.
30. Francis Bacon in conversation with Melvyn Bragg, BBC interview, 1966.
31. These are the ambitions set down in the original proposals for the chapel.
32. Ghislaine also organised photography and drawing workshops with the women and children in the Refuge, and her activities here and elsewhere have contributed to her being named as a 'Woman of the Year' in 2009 and later receiving an 'Excellence in the Community' award in 2010.
33. Four suicide bombers carried out an attack in central London on Thursday 7 July, killing 52 people and injuring more than 770 others.
34. Adam Bambury, *Interview*: *Ghislaine Howard discusses the 365 Series at Imperial War Museum*

North, Culture24.org.uk, 27 February 2009. https://www.wikiwand.com/en/Imperial_War_Museum_North.

35. Jim Forrester, 'War & Conflict: New Perspectives in the North', *Manchester Region History Review*, Vol. 17 No. 1, Manchester Metropolitan University, 2004.

36. Mat Collishaw's *Last Meal On Death Row* series is a sequence of photographs set up with great skill to imitate the formal qualities of Dutch seventeenth-century still-life painting. At first sight they are easily mistaken as examples of that genre, but on closer inspection they reveal themselves as modern-day meals. We have to read the information panels to learn that their subject is actually the last meals of condemned prisoners in American prisons.

37. Emily Dickinson, letter, probably to Sally Bowles, L 251, she continues, 'when your thought wavers, for such a foot as mine'. Cristanne Miller, *Emily Dickinson, A Poet's Grammar*, Harvard University Press, 1987, p.11.

38. One of the most engaging and community-minded individuals in Glossopdale is the multi-talented Sean Wood, artist, musician and nature writer – not to mention a brilliant cook – who runs a quite extraordinary café gallery in Padfield, just a mile or so away from Glossop. Ghislaine is patron of two charities, Crossroads Derbyshire and Parkinsons Equip.

39. Philip Larkin, *Required Writing: Miscellaneous Pieces 1955–1982*, Faber & Faber, 1983, quoted in Lawrence Coupe, *Myth*, Routledge, 1997, p.11.

40. William Shakespeare, *Hamlet*, c.1598–1602, Act 1, Scene 2 and Act 3, Scene 2.

41. 'I shall give a proof to demonstrate with facts that there are no rules in painting and that the tyranny which obliges everyone, as if they were slaves, to study in the same way or to follow the same method is a great impediment to the young who practise this very difficult art, which comes closer to the divine than any other, since it makes known what God has created.' Francisco Goya, letter of 14 October 1792 to Bernardo de Iriarte, Vice-Protector of the Academia Real de San Fernando, Madrid. Cited in Enriqueta Harris, *Goya*, Phaidon, 1994, p.24.

42. On 22 October, 1907, the Austrian poet Rainer Maria Rilke wrote to his wife of Cézanne's *Portrait of Madame Cézanne*, c. 1886. 'It's as if every part were aware of all the others—it participates that much; that much adjustment and rejection is happening in it; that's how each daub plays its part in maintaining equilibrium and in producing it: just as the whole picture finally keeps reality in equilibrium.'

43. Rainer Maria Rilke's sonnet 'Blue Hydrangea' was written in 1906, the year of Cézanne's death, and appears in his collection, *New Poems*. In his review of the Impressionist exhibition of 1880,

J-K Huysmans claimed that no other painter after Delacroix 'has understood as M. Degas has the marriage and adultery of colours.' A phrase that has always appealed to Ghislaine.

44. Pliny (61–c. 113), *Naturalis Historia* XXXV, lines 143–6, written (c. 77–79 AD), see Pliny. *Natural History in Ten Volumes*. Volume IX, Libri XXXIII–XXXV (The Loeb Classical Library) Harvard University Press, 1968.

45. Ghislaine Howard, *Artists & Illustrators* Magazine, October 1992.

46. John Ruskin, *Elements of Drawing*, first published in 1857, the illustrated edition with notes by Bernard Dunstan, is both informative and beautiful, published by The Herbert Press in 1991. In his autobiography, *Praeterita*, first published in 1899. This section was written in 1886, remembering an event that had taken place over forty years earlier, in 1842. He was in the Forest of Fontainebleau drawing the delicate forms of an aspen tree. 'Languidly, but not idly, I began to draw it; and as I drew, the languor passed away: the beautiful lines insisted on being traced — without weariness. More and more beautiful they became, as each rose out of the rest, and took its place in the air. With wonder increasing every instant, I saw that they "composed" themselves, by finer laws than any known of men. At last, the tree was there, and everything that I had thought before about trees, nowhere!' *Praeterita* II, Alfred A. Knopf, 2005, pp.277–8.

47. Rudolf Arnheim, *Art and Visual Perception: A Psychology of the Creative Eye*, University of California Press, 1974, [first published 1954], p.5.

48. Wallace Stevens, 'Thirteen Ways of Looking at a Blackbird', V.

49. Claude Monet writing to Gustave Geffroy on 11 August 1908, quoted in Michael Howard, *The Impressionists by Themselves*, Conran Octopus, 1991, p.299.

50. *Artist & Illustrators* Magazine, October, 2008.

51. Extracts from Ghislaine's Journal were published in *Art Review*, March 1994 as 'An Artist's Diary'.

52. Extracts for David Peters Corbett's essay for 'A Shared Experience', Manchester Art Gallery, 1993.

53. Emma L.E. Rees, *The Vagina: A Literary and Cultural History,* Bloomsbury Publishing, 2013 and Claire Harbottle, 'Lilla's Birthing: Re-appropriating the Subjective Experience of Birthing in Visual Art' at http://claireharbottlebirthwork.blogspot.co.uk/p/visual-representation-of-birth-paper.html.

54. Ezra Pound, 'A Retrospect' an essay in *Pavannes and Divagations*, first published in 1918.

55. Hannah Rothschild, *The Daily Telegraph*, 'Frank Auerbach: An interview with one of our greatest living painters', 30 September 2013.

56. Quoted in Maurice Sérullaz, *L'univers de Degas,* H. Scrépel, 1979, p.13.

57. C. P. Cavafy's exquisite poem, 'The Old Mirror in

the Hall', expresses this idea perfectly.

58. Ghislaine delights in remembering how one of her teacher nuns would tell of her sister, who was miraculously saved from the sinking Titanic by being blown out of the ship's funnel and landing miraculously in a nearby life-boat!

59. Most famously it was Cézanne identified with the Frenhofer, Balzac's fictional *artiste-maudit*, who is the central character of his 1831 novella, *Le Chef-d'oeuvre inconnu*, (*The Unknown Masterpiece*). Like so many artists, including Picasso, Duchamp, de Kooning and more recently, Richard Hamilton, Ghislaine has been both intrigued and troubled by this compelling tale of artistic failure.

60. Dr. Helen Bamber, OBE (1925–2014). In 1945, aged 20, she was part of a small relief unit sent to work in the recently liberated former concentration camp of Bergen-Belsen; she continued to work tirelessly in the human rights field for more than 60 years, helping thousands of survivors worldwide. In 1985 she founded The Medical Foundation for the Care of Victims of Torture and in 2005 she founded her own charity – the Helen Bamber Foundation.

61. Laura Gascoigne, *Death's Broken Dominion, The Tablet*, April, 2008.

62. *Edouard Manet, Souvenirs*, Paris: H. Laurens, 1913, as quoted in Juliet Wilson-Bareau, *Manet by Himself*, Little, Brown and Co., 1991, p.136.

63. 'What Kind of Times Are These?' From Bertholt Brecht, 'For Those Born Later' (An Die Nachgeborenen) – taken by Adrienne Rich for her poem of the same title.

64. T. S. Eliot, 'Burnt Norton', first poem of the 'Four Quartets', published as a whole in 1943; W. H. Auden, 'Musée des Beaux Arts', was composed in December 1938.

65. Goya created these etchings and aquatints between 1810 and 1820. They are records of his impassioned response to the Spanish struggle against the French army under Napoleon Bonaparte, who invaded Spain in 1808.

66. Edgar Degas in conversation with Georges Jeanniot, *Souvenirs sur Degas*, (*Memories of Degas*), 1933.

67. Primo Levi, *The Drowned and the Saved*, trans. Raymond Rosenthal, Vintage Books, 1989, pp. 83–4.

68. W. B. Yeats, 'Before the World Was Made'. One of his many elegiac poems that deal with the loss of innocence that comes with age and self-scrutiny.

69. The masters – an unfortunate term, but the alternative is hardly better. It is interesting that Ghislaine has rarely copied the work of Berthe Morisot whose work has had such a powerful impact upon her. She has also learnt much from such contemporary women artists as Marlene Dumas, Cecily Brown and Eileen Cooper.

70. Picasso, in a statement made to Marius de Zayas,

Footnotes Continued

1923, 'Picasso Speaks,' *The Arts*, New York, May 1923, pp.315–26; reprinted in Alfred Barr: Picasso, New York 1946, pp.270–1.

71. Edgar Degas, as quoted by George Moore, in his 'Memories of Degas' , the *Burlington Magazine*, January and February, 1918.

72. Alfredo Casella, *Music in my Time*, translated and edited by Spencer Norton, University of Oklahoma Press, 1955, p. 87.

73. As quoted in the *London Magazine*, February 1962, which featured two of Sylvia Plath's poems and printed the responses of twenty-six writers to a number of questions under the title: 'Context'.

74. As quoted in Lou Kennedy, *Business Etiquette for the Nineties: Your Ticket to Career Success*,1992, p.8.

75. Hannah Rothschild, *The Daily Telegraph*, 'Frank Auerbach: An interview with one of our greatest living painters', 30 September 2013.

76. T. S. Eliot, '*Ulysses*, Order, and Myth,' *The Dial*, 1923, pp.482–3.

77. One example will suffice to illustrate this point: 'If you wish to get hold of the invisible, you must penetrate as deeply as possible into the visible. My aim is to get hold of the magic reality and to transform this reality into painting. ... It is reality which forms the mystery of our existence.' Max Beckmann, quoting 'the famous kabbalist' (whom he neglects to name), in his address given on the occasion of the *Exhibition of 20th Century German Art* at the New Burlington Galleries in London, on 21 July 1938. Quoted in Barbara Copeland Buenger, (ed.), *Max Beckmann: Self-Portrait in Words*, University of Chicago Press, 1997, p.302.

78. The exhibition 'The Circus Animals' Desertion', took place in 2010 in Birr, County Offaly as part of their Arts Festival in 2010. For a much more extensive, and incisive, discussion of the significance of Picasso for Ghislaine's work in relation to Yeats's 'The Circus Animals' Desertion', see Michael Howard, 'Feasting with Giants: The Impact of Yeats and Picasso on Ghislaine Howard's Recent Work' in *The Circus Animals' Desertion: paintings, drawings and prints by Ghislaine Howard made in response to the poetry of W. B. Yeats*, 2010, pp.8–15.

79. Dorothea Tanning, *Between Lives: an Artist and her World*, W.W. Norton and Company, 2001, pp.62–3.

80. Evelyn Underhill, *Mysticism: A Study in Nature and Development of Spiritual Consciousness*, Methuen & co., 1911, p.278.

81. Charles Baudelaire, 'Salon of 1846', in *Art in Paris 1845–1862*, edited and translated by Jonathan Mayne, Phaidon, 1965, p. 119.

82. A piece of writing taken from one of my sketchbooks.

83. Quoted many times, this version was transcribed from notes taken by his biographer, Shelley Rohde.

84. Sister Wendy Beckett chose Ghislaine's work to represent her choice of artist in the 1992 Bruton Street Gallery exhibition, *Women Critics Choose Women Painters*. We could interpret this term in a number of ways, but perhaps the most pertinent is the meaning associated with psychoanalytic theory, in which Eros, the 'life force' is opposed by the destructive death instinct of Thanatos.

85. Joachim Gasquet, P. M. Doran (ed.), *Conversations avec Cézanne*, Collection Macula, 1978, pp.108–109. As Cézanne once asserted, colour is 'the place where our brain and the universe meet'. Evan Thompson, *Colour Vision: A Study in Cognitive Science and the Philosophy of Perception*, Routledge, 1995, pp.4–10.

86. Emmanuel Levinas, *Totality and Infinity*, trans. A. Lingis Duquesne University Press, 1969, p.142. See also John Sallis, "Levinas and the Elemental", in *Research in Phenomenology*, 28 (1998), p.158.

87. *Bemerkungen über die Farben*, (*Remarks on Colour*) was one of Ludwig Wittgenstein's last works In which he returns to some of ideas on colour and vision that he had wrestled with in his earliest philosophical work, the famous *Tractatus Philosophico-Mathematicus*,, published 1921. Wittgenstein told his friend Norman Malcolm, 'It's partly boring and repelling, but in some ways also very instructive philosophically. . . . it stimulates me to think'. Cited in Ray Monk, Ludwig Wittgenstein: *The Duty of Genius,* Vintage, 1990, pp.561.

88. Quoted letter from Tony Marshall's letter, artist's correspondence.

89. Lesley Sutton, *PassionArt Trail: Be Still*, Manchester Cathedral and other Manchester city venues, exhibition catalogue, February–April, 2016.

90. Ben Okri, *Birds of Heaven*, Orion, 1995, p.1.

91. Andrei Tarkovsky wrote of a portrait by Leonardo, 'We shall derive deep pleasure from the realisation that we cannot exhaust it, nor see to the end of it. A true artistic image gives the beholder a simultaneous experience of the most complex, contradictory, sometimes even mutually exclusive feelings.' Andrei Tarkovsky, *Sculpting in Time*, translated by Kitty Hunter Blair, University of Texas Press, 1983, p.109.

92. Though the exhibition was entitled 'Women and Men', the catalogue, written by its curator Sarah Hyde, was entitled *Exhibiting Gender*, published by Manchester University Press,1997.

Selected Public Exhibitions

A Shared Experience, solo exhibition, Manchester City Art Gallery, resulting from a six-month residency in Saint Mary's Maternity Unit, Manchester, April—May 1993.
Caught in The Act: Paintings produced as the official painter to Manchester's year as 'European City of Drama', British Council, Manchester, November, September 1994.
'The Women of Troy' Paintings and Drawings, National Theatre, London, June 1995.
The Informal Portrait, Whitworth Art Gallery, University of Manchester, November–January 1997–8.
Ghislaine Howard: Recent Work, solo exhibition, Horizon Modern Art, Brussels, November 1998.
The Discerning Eye, London, November 1998.
The Stations of the Cross / The Captive Figure, Liverpool Cathedrals, April–May 2000.
Times of Our Lives, Endings and *Beginnings*, Whitworth Art Gallery, University of Manchester, April–October 2000.
Exhibition in Aid of the Medical Foundation Caring for Victims of Torture, Royal College of Art, London, October 2000.
Stations of the Cross / The Captive Figure, The Chapter House, Canterbury Cathedral, March 2001.
The Captive Figure, The Cynthia Corbett Gallery at 54, The Gallery, London, March 2001.
Intimacy, Mostyn Gallery, Llandudno and The Lowry, Salford, January–28 April 2002.
The Stations of the Cross / The Captive Figure, Liverpool Cathedral, March–April 2002.
Presence, Saint Paul's Cathedral, London, February 2004.
A Shared Experience, The Sheridan Russell Gallery, London, September 2004.
Vesali Icones, paintings included as the setting for Sir Peter Maxwell Davies's *Vesali Icones* with the musical ensemble *Psappha*, the Gulbenkian, Lisbon, January 2005, Queen Elizabeth Hall, May 2005, Buenos Aires, June 2005.
The Stations of The Cross / The Captive Figure, Liverpool Cathedral, for Liverpool Capital of Culture, including a commissioned piece, *The Empty Tomb*, February–March 2008.
The 365 Series, Imperial War Museum North, March 2009.
The Circus Animals' Desertion, Birr Arts Festival, Ireland, August 2010.
The Choreography of Walking, Chapman Gallery, Salford University, March 2011.
The Stations of the Cross / The Captive Figure, York Minster, February–May 2012.
Ice Age Art / Arrival of the Modern Mind, The British Museum, March–June 2013.
Return of the Prodigal Son, Manchester Cathedral, July–September 2015.
Young Masters – Dialogues, Sphinx Fine Art in association with The Cynthia Corbett Gallery, October 2015.
Be Still, John Rylands Library February–April 2016.

Selected Publications

'Artist's Diary,' *Art Review*, March 1994.
British Museum, Ice Age Art; The Female Gaze, 2013
Corbett, David Peters, *A Shared Experience*, (exhibition catalogue), Manchester City Art Gallery and Wellcome Foundation, 1993/4.
Davis, Peter, *A Northern School Revisited*, Clark Art Ltd., 2015.
Doney, Meryl, *Presence*, (exhibition catalogue), St. Paul's Cathedral, London, 2004.
Gascoigne, Laura, *Death's Broken Dominion*, *The Tablet*, March 2008.
Gascoigne, Laura, *The Tablet*, April 2014.
Harbottle, Claire, 'Lilla's Birthing: Re-appropriating the Subjective Experience of Birthing in Visual Art' at:
http://claireharbottlebirthwork.blogspot.co.uk/p/visual-representation-of-birth-paper.html.
Howard, Michael, *Circus Animals' Desertion*, Irish Arts Council, 2010.
Howard, Michael, *Stations of the Cross / The Captive Figure*, with contributions by Joan Crossley and Shannon Ledbetter, Liverpool Hope University, 2000.
Hyde, Sarah, *Exhibiting Gender*, (exhibition catalogue), Whitworth Art Gallery, Manchester University Press, 1997.
Smith, Ray Campbell, *Drawing Figures* and *Portraiture*, Dorling Kindersley in association with the Royal Academy, 1994, 1999.
Nagle, Frances, *Steeplechase Park*, Rockingham Press, 2004.
Rees, Emma L. E., *The Vagina: A Literary and Cultural History,* Bloomsbury Publishing, 2013.
Regan, Martin, *The Northern School, A Reappraisal*, Gateway Gallery, 2016.
Rose, Judy, *Twelve Women Artists*, Wendy Levy Contemporary Art, 2006.
Sutton, Lesley, (ed.), *PassionArt*, 2014.
Wollen, Roger, *A Guide to the Methodist Art Collection*, Trustees of the Methodist Church Collection of Modern Christian Art, 2002.

Ghislaine in the Picture Store, Glossop
2016
Photograph by Micah Purnell

Michael and Pip in the Kitchen, Glossop
2016
Photograph by Micah Purnell

The Studio, Glossop
2016
Photograph by Micah Purnell

Acknowledgments and Thanks

We want first of all to thank Martin Heaps, whose vision, generosity and support have made this book possible. We would also like to thank Penny Macbeth, Dean of Manchester School of Art. It is a great privilege to be associated with such a hive of creative and critical activity. We were fortunate too, to find in Micah Purnell, a book designer of real flair, understanding and discernment. His engagement with Ghislaine's work has created a truly illuminating synthesis of word and image. Also crucial to this enterprise was the keen-eye of Adrian Lambert, whose photography has caught the full richness and texture of Ghislaine's work – no easy task. A special thank you also to Martin Regan, whose belief in Ghislaine's work has never wavered.

Thanks must also go to our friends and colleagues, who have also encouraged us in different ways in what has been an exciting, and on occasion, emotionally demanding project. Too many to mention individually, but particular thanks must be offered to: Rebecca Anderton, Fionna Barber, Sophie Benson, Steph Boydell, Kathy Bruce, Jill Cook, Aiden Cross, Joan Crossley, Susan Eyres, Brian Fell, Raffi Der Haroutunian, Thom Hetherington, Cordelia Howard, Max Howard, Kate Jessen, Christine Keddle, Shannon Ledbetter, Chris and Julie McCabe, Jane Matthews, Katherine Miller, Sam Milsom, Ian Mood, Andrea May, Alastair Noble, Peter Ogilvie, Anna Paterson, David Peters Corbett, Rachel Pugh, Bill Robb, John Sheeran, Michael Simpson, Claire Stewart, Kenelm and Karen Storey, Lesley Sutton, Virginia Tandy, Sean Wood, (not least for second-guessing the book's title!), Stephen Yates for his photographs of the 365 Series, Saltwick Nab and Flamborough Head.

We would also like to express our appreciation to the many private collectors who have allowed their works to be photographed and reproduced.

Ghislaine Howard;
The Human Touch:
Paintings, drawings and prints: 1980–2016
By Michael Howard

ghislainehoward.com
info@ghislainehoward.com
m.howard928@btinternet.com

Manchester Metropolitan University
in association with Martin Heaps
martin@collectart.co.uk
collectart.co.uk

First published in 2017

A catalogue reference for this book is available
from the British Library

ISBN 978-1-910029-26-8

Printed in England using paper from responsible sources.

© 2017

Art Direction, Design & Cover Design
Micah Purnell
micahpurnell.com | twitter @micahpurnell

Photography
Adrian Lambert
adrianlambertphotography.co.uk | adrian@lambert.photo

Editors
Michael Howard, Ghislaine Howard & Micah Purnell